Customizing Your Harley

TAB | TAB BOOKS
Blue Ridge Summit, PA

Customiz

HARLEY

Carl Caiati

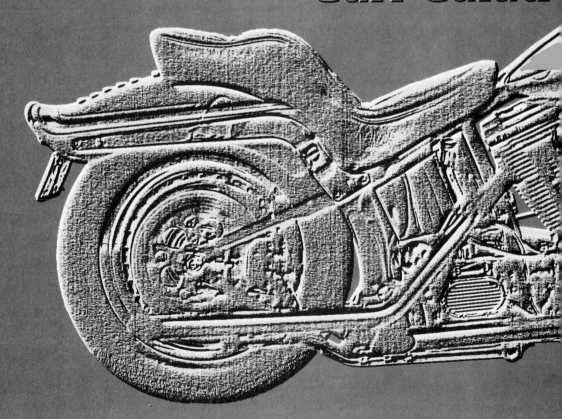

ing Your

To the sweet little Cathy Sue Freeze,
My clipped-wing bird in the ungilded cage,
with much affection.

FIRST EDITION
FIRST PRINTING

©1993 by **TAB Books**.
TAB Books is a division of McGraw-Hill, Inc.

Library of Congress Cataloging-in-Publication Data
Caiati, Carl.
    Customizing your Harley / by Carl Caiati.
        p.   cm.
    Includes index.
    ISBN 0-8306-4118-1 (hard) ISBN 0-8306-4117-3 (paper)
    1. Harley-Davidson motorcycle—Customizing.   I. Title.
TL448.H3C34   1992
629.227'5—dc20   92-11140
                                     CIP

Acquisitions editor: Stacey V. Pomeroy
Editorial team: Joanne Slike, Executive Editor
                Steve Messner, Editor
                Jodi L. Tyler, Indexer
Production team: Katherine G. Brown, Director of Production
                Jana Fisher, Layout
                Nadine McFarland, Quality Control
                Nancy Mickley, Proofreader
Design team: Jaclyn J. Boone, Designer
              Brian Allison, Associate Designer
Cover design: Sandra Blair Design, Harrisburg, Pa.   HT1

Acknowledgments

This book required not only many hours of work but also assistance from customizers and accessory manufacturers, most of whom contributed unstintingly to help me put this manual together.

First and foremost I would like to thank Ron Finch of Finch's Custom Styled Cycles in Pontiac, Michigan. Our association goes back many years. Not only was Ron my mentor, he also taught me the fine art of motorcycle painting and fabrication. Although we approach motorcycle customizing in different fashions, his influence shows in my work. Ron also provided some of the excellent, second-to-none artistic customs shown within these pages.

Dave Perowitz, another premier custom bike builder from Brockton, Massachusetts, also provided help generously and cooperatively, allowing me to feature some of his inimitable creations, which aesthetically enhance the value of this book.

Harley-Davidson via one of their PR people, Dan Klemencik, also came through with some required photos and data. "Mr. Harley-Davidson," Phil Peterson of Peterson's Harley-Davidson, Miami, Florida, was as gracious as only he can be. Mention Harley and Phil is always ready, willing, and able to help. Peterson's manager, Ace Armstrong, another great provider, was there donating expertise, bikes, whatever. Larry Stanley of "Heaven on Wheels," Ft. Lauderdale, Florida, also shared some how-to expertise. Bob Davis of Red Racing, Boca Raton, Florida, was responsible for the superlative plating and welding metalwork by his crew in the chapter on frames. Ron Paugh of Paughco gave me a fair share of his time, providing not only valuable product photos but also the frame we glorified in chapter 2. Tom Motzco of Drag Specialties was also on the bandwagon with photos and parts, as was Amy Bahr of Custom Chrome.

Brothers III of Pompano Beach, Florida, provided some good show bikes and allowed me to borrow and photograph some parts. Thanks also go to Colin and Rocky of Brothers, as well as to Frenchy for his fiberglass expertise and hours of general reminiscing.

Last but not least, I thank styling genius Wyatt Fuller, the "Prince of Parts," for his unlimited creations, avant-garde accessories distributed and marketed by Kuryakin, a new company that Wyatt hopes will properly market and make available to a desiring public his great, innovative parts.

Kirk Van Scoten is the owner and president of Sumax, a company that is a boon to the accessory and decorative field. Kirk gave many hours of his time, provided very important data and photos, and proved to be a valuable colleague.

To all who generously contributed, I bestow my profound gratitude.

CONTENTS

CARL CAIATI is as unique and individually American as Harley-Davidson itself. The son of a key member of the New York Philharmonic Symphony, Carl was winning prestigious awards for photojournalism when most men and women his age came no closer to art and publishing than their high school yearbooks.

But his rough-and-tumble youth on the streets of the Bronx gravitated him to the unpretentiousness of motorcycling, where the machines and the people were real. It was an ideal match for his artistic talents, flair for the dramatic, and quick grasp of technicalities. There were few in the industry who could research, build, write, and photograph the subject at such a consistently outstanding professional level. Carl has done it all— from how-tos on his own bike projects to color cover and centerspread photo features in leading motorcycle and automotive magazines. His mural and graphic painting ranked with the best, and his first book on custom painting, which he wrote over a decade ago, is still a best-seller.

I got to know Carl when we were both freelance writers and photographers for the motorcycle magazines of the late 1960s. These were the early and halcyon days of motorcycle customizing, when most parts had to be made, not bought, and when many modifications meant researching the unknown. Carl was always generous with his time, knowledge, and encouragement for friends who needed it. Thanks to him, customizers such as Ron Finch gained richly deserved national exposure for their work, and motorcycle customizing grew from an obscure cult to a worldwide trend. And thanks in no small part to Carl's tutelage, I went on to magazine staff positions in this growing industry, including a stint at *Easyriders* magazine.

Today, Carl's youthful genius has matured and his exuberance has been tempered by experience as he has reached his fifth decade on the planet. Readers of this contemporary custom manual can be the beneficiaries of a breadth of seasoned talent and knowledge that is truly rare on the American scene.

Sandy "Jake" Roca

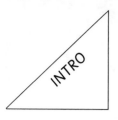
INTRO

The case for customizing

THE HARLEY-DAVIDSON motorcycle, as American as apple pie, has come to the forefront in the 1990s as the most coveted, most acclaimed, most favored motorcycle of the decade.

Many riders keep their machines in showroom stock condition, satisified with the Harley's unique style. But a large contingent of Harley owners prefers a bike that is individualized, one that reflects the owner's character and personality, and doesn't look like everybody else's. Individualizing your bike, making it an art form and a statement of self-expression, is what this book is all about.

For many years, Harleys served just as functional motorcycles. But in the early 1960s, serious bike buffs began changing them to suit their particular requirements—aesthetic or otherwise. Smaller tanks and leaner looks were in vogue; lighter weight for better performance and handling was another consideration. Bikers began to modify, cut, and chop, and the "chopper" was born. The true chopper enjoyed great popularity for over a decade, but soon gave way to the more streetable, more comfortable, better-handling street custom that prevails today. Current Harley-Davidson models are based on the traditional lowrider configuration, though a few street dressers, cruisers, and the popular new Fat Boy are also marketed.

One of the key figures involved in the evolution of the lowrider was Arlen Ness. A serious bike builder who first started altering and modifying his own Knucklehead, Ness incorporated metalwork and design features that made the custom bike world notice—and then emulate—the styling. Ness basically created what is known today as the "Bay Area Lowrider." This style incorporates long, low, lean lines and mildly raked front forks. The true lowrider displays swayed-back lines, low frame setup, and low slimline seating for a forward, racy look. Today, Ness owns Arlen Ness Enterprises, San Leandro, California, a custom accessories supplier

Prominent also in the 1960s was Ron Finch, who elevated the custom chopper to metal-sculpture art with his avant-garde creations. Finch's work has graced not only the pages of custom motorcycle magazines but the floors of the Detroit Art

Museum and other distinguished national and international museums. Though lowriders predominate today, choppers still survive, particularly in show bike circles. It's a matter of personal choice as to which way the customizer wishes to go. Some Harleys, such as the Super Glides—which themselves emulate the lowrider—can be considered factory customs, a theme chosen by Harley-Davidson. One look even dates back to the early hardtail styling; the Heritage Softail recreates the stylish lines of the 1949 hardtail Hydra-Glide, but with a specially formulated rear suspension system built into the design of the frame.

How does one go about designing and building a custom motorcycle? The main objective is to interject your own ideas and personality into your customizing plans. If you don't already own one, when you go out to purchase your Harley, choose a model whose design is most closely styled and suited to your taste. It is always easier to make variations and modifications to an existing theme.

After you have decided what type of bike you want to build (for example, a dresser, chopper, lowrider, cafe racer, and so on), peruse the pages of custom motorcycle magazines such as *American Iron*, *Easyriders*, *Hot Bike*, and *Supercycle* (to name only a few) and start creating your dream bike on paper. Select the features you desire and add them to a drawing or paste-up, which should begin with the frame and wheels. Find pictures of bare frames to photocopy or trace in catalogs offered by Paughco, Inc., Sumax, Drag Specialties, Custom Chrome, Inc. (CCI), and other suppliers of custom accessories. These catalogs also illustrate parts you might want to trace onto your mockup drawing. You must also decide whether the custom parts you wish to add can be mounted on your style bike. The catalogs will specify which are bolt-on items for your particular bike or frame (as most are), universal mount units, or components that will need to be adapted in order for them to be mounted. (See the Appendix for suppliers' addresses.)

For those of you with limited sketching experience, you can cut out catalog or magazine photos of parts and fashion a structural collage on paper. If you prefer to go the bolt-on accessory route, the catalogs will show you what parts are available for your style Harley, what is exchangeable, and what is adaptable. The catalogs will also show style trends for such items as handlebars, seats, footpegs, engine side covers, sissy rails, fenders, handgrips, tanks, fairings, saddlebags, and so on.

Scale mockups are another route for designing your custom. Your local hobby shop will most likely stock an assortment of plastic Harley-Davidson motorcycle models. There should be a kit for every model to date. With these kits you can mix, match, swap, and custom-fabricate in scale the parts or styling differences you wish to incorporate into your Harley. You can also experiment with paint scheme alternatives and see how they work on a three-dimensional basis. I myself have built some street customs based on preliminary scale-model experimenting.

Once you have determined what look or style you desire, buy the parts and add them on, or let your dealer do it for you. It's cheaper and more fun to do it yourself, though, and most custom-fashioned parts marketed today can be easily installed with simple tools such as screwdrivers, drills, and socket wrenches.

If you want a good-riding, good-handling street custom, *do not* alter the frame rake or suspension. If you wish to chop or make radical modifications, study the recommendations made in chapter 2. The look you wish to give your bike is solely up to you, based on the components you select to modify and complete the entire aesthetic package.

This book should prove valuable to all do-it-yourself custom builders, whether you wish to build a simple bolt-on or a radical custom package. Included in this volume are pertinent hints and tips for both degrees of customizing, as well as a list of sources for parts and accessories you will need in creating your own unique set of wheels.

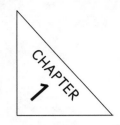

Harley-Davidson models & engines

SINCE ITS INCEPTION in 1903, the Harley-Davidson Motor Company, initially formed by William Harley and Arthur, Walter, and William Davidson, has generated a host of quality motorcycles. Distinctive, classic styling coupled with spirited performance make today's Harley-Davidsons the most sought-after bikes. Harley reigns as the Rolls-Royce of two-wheelers, generating unprecedented sales among enthusiasts who range from blue-collar workers to business executives and Hollywood celebrities. Such notables include Dan Akroyd, the late Malcolm Forbes, Reggie Jackson, Olivia Newton-John, Ken Norton, Sylvester Stallone, Burt Reynolds, and the list goes on. Unique and distinctive, Harley-Davidsons are the only truly mass-produced, all-American motorcycles made today.

In the early decades of production, Harley-Davidson sales reached a peak in 1926 when 23,354 cycles were sold; this figure would not be exceeded until 1942.

Many Harley-Davidson motorcycles and Servi-cars built from 1929 to 1951 were powered by the classic 45-cubic inch (c.i.) V-twin (Fig. 1-1). The early engines (designated R) remained the same up to 1936. A low-compression D model (for sidecar model bikes), a standard DL model, and a higher compression DLD model were the three optional engines offered.

Harley 45

1-1
The WLA-45 was an early production Harley-Davidson engine. This unit, from the collection of Larry Stanley, is a 1942 model.

Harley-Davidson models & engines 1

A few 45 engines are still around, mostly in restorations or Servi-Cars; a few customs exist that feature rebuilt 45s. The W series 45 engines also rated high in motorcycle racing until production ceased in 1951.

Not predominating in custom circles, 45-powered bikes, stock and custom modified, still retain their charisma, though mainly due to their collectibility and the nostalgia they create.

Knucklehead   Another dated but desirable Harley engine is the Knucklehead. Introduced in 1936, it was Harley-Davidson's first production overhead valve (OHV) V-twin. Displacing 61 c.i., the Knucklehead engine featured a hemispherical head and a revolutionary (at the time), highly efficient recirculating oil system (Fig. 1-2). An improved Knucklehead version was introduced in 1941. Displacement was increased to 74 c.i. Another major improvement in the Knucklehead was an upgraded clutch featuring three steel and three fiber discs together with a spring disk providing smoother, more positive shifting. Because of its classic looks and excellent reliability, Knuckleheads are in demand by collectors and customizers alike.

1-2
A vintage Knucklehead motor powers Todd Schuster's Spider. Knuckles are rare, but still coveted by custom and chopper buffs.

The year 1948 found Harley-Davidson incorporating some Major changes beginning with the introduction of the Panhead engine. (Figs. 1-3 and 1-4). The Panhead featured 61 c.i. (EL) or 74 c.i. displacement. Superceding the Knucklehead, the Panhead provided better oil control and was lighter in weight due to the new aluminum cylinder heads. The OHV Panheads used pushrod-type hydraulic lifters and featured redesigned heads and rocker arms. The newer lifters minimized tappet noise, and the new heads dissipated heat better.

Panhead

1-3
Another of Larry Stanley's collectibles, this classic 1965 1200cc Panhead experienced a long Harley life, spanning a few decades.

1-4
Though nearly lost in the glamour and glitter, a refined 1956 Panhead powers Wild Child, an award-winning custom seen on the custom show circuit.

The Panhead enjoyed a long life, cradled in the famous hardtail frame. It became the driving force of the Hydra-Glide in 1949, the Duo Glide in 1958, and the Electra Glide as late as 1965, the last Harley to feature the Panhead engine. The classic springer fork was deleted in favor of hydraulic front forks, a feature that would soon become a standard in future Harley and competitive brand motorcycles.

In 1952, the 61 c.i. EL model was discontinued. The 74 c.i. FL model was an optional foot shift. The FLH was introduced in 1955. The FLH featured stronger main bearings. Electric start was added in 1965.

The FLH is still sought after for customizing, and respected and coveted by custom Harley buffs. There's an old adage: "Old Panheads never die; they just get rebuilt."

Shovelhead

The Shovelhead engine is still popular and thousands of them still power stock and custom bikes. Making its debut in 1966, the Shovelhead was to become the primary engine for the next two decades (Fig. 1-5). The first Shovelheads displaced 74 c.i. The 80 c.i. Shovelhead was first offered in 1978, but the 74 was still available through 1980. A V-twin like its predecessor, the stock FLH Shovelhead produced 5 hp more than the Panhead. The newly designed engine exhibited less vibration and was equipped with the new Tillotson diaphragm carburetor.

1-5
This early '70s street chopper by Mardo Bennett features a Shovelhead top end and Panhead bottom end. This type of swapping was common in the 1960s and 1970s.

The FLH Shovelhead was rated at 60 hp, with the FL Shovelhead rated at 54 hp.

Other major improvements were instituted in the FLH, FL, and consecutive models. In 1967, a push-pull choke was added. An improved oil pump became standard in 1968, and special warning lights were added to indicate oil, generator, and ignition conditions. In 1970, serrated header pipe covers were omitted in favor of chrome headers and the generator was replaced by an alternator.

Other Shovelhead-powered models were the FX Glides, the Super Glides, and the FXS Low Rider. The 80 c.i. Shovelhead also powered the 1980 FLT Tour Glide, which offered Harley's first five-speed gearbox and the new V-Fire CD ignition system. In 1981 the V-Fire became the V-Fire II system.

Another Super Glide version premiering in 1980 was the FXB Sturgis, the B indicating belt-drive. The belt-type driveline required no lubrication, lasted longer, and ran quieter than conventional sprocket-chain drive. The last Shovelhead-powered Harleys were made in the latter part of 1984.

Sportster V-Twin

The XL Sportster was introduced in 1957. The light and powerful Sportster has been one of Harley-Davidson's best-selling models ever since (Figs. 1-6 and 1-7).

1-6
Here's a close-to-stock Sportster of the mid-1970s set up as a street machine. The engine has a 69-cubic-inch displacement.

Harley-Davidson models & engines 5

1-7
The lean, long look indicative of '70s choppers is seen here, sporting a 1972 XLCH engine, raked front end, and high sissy rail. Customizing is by Jack Thomas of Long Island, New York.

The first XL owed its unexcelled performance to its responsive OHV system. The 1958 Sportster featured added performance with its F and X series engines. The F series sported a swing-arm frame with auto-type shock absorbers. This Sportster model was designated the Duo Glide. The X and SLCH Sportsters differed in being magneto equipped. Changes for 1962 included short, staggered dual exhausts, and the fork brackets and motor mounts were refashioned of aluminum.

In 1964, aluminum front wheel hubs became standard on all Sportster models. In 1965 the electrical system was upped to 12 volts. In 1968 the magneto system was scrapped and the kick starter swapped for the electric starter. By 1968, the hot XLCH twin was capable of producing 58 hp at 6800 rpm. The front fork again was altered to upgrade handling. The change from a dry to a wet clutch was made in 1971; in order to simplify timing adjustments, the timer was set into the cam cover (Fig. 1-8).

The XLCR Cafe Racer premiered in 1977 to broaden Sportster appeal, and it generated some interest for two consecutive years. In 1979 the Ham Can air cleaner was discarded and replaced with the more conservative looking "breadbox" air cleaner.

1-8
Close-up view of the XLCH engine that was typical of the mid-1970 issues. Sporties then featured large batteries and side-mounted oil tanks.

Appearing in 1979 was the XLS Roadster with lowrider styling. The XLS featured a 16-inch rear tire, and a Hugger model offered low seating made possible by shorter shock absorbers.

In 1983, a no-frills XLX was offered, as well as a limited-production XR1000. Up to and including 1985, Harley-Davidson offered three Sportster models: the XLX, the XR1000, and the regular Sportster, all featuring an improved, upgraded 1000cc motor.

In 1986, the XR1000 was dropped from the roster, superceded by the new Sportster 1100 XLH. Also premiering that year was the 883cc Evolution-powered XLH, replacing the XLX.

Evolution series

The Evolution series Harleys, featuring the revolutionary Evolution engine first introduced in 1984, are dominating the American bike scene. The Evolution is favored over competitive offerings, as it is less prone to leak oil and virtually trouble-free. Also popular is its famed 45-degree V-twin engine configuration and its highly efficient five-speed gearbox (Fig. 1-9).

1-9

Bob Marlino's Evolution street wheel epitomizes the 1980s lowrider fat-bob look that is currently both desirable and fashionable.

The Softail Harley model was the first to feature the Evolution in 1984, but the entire Harley line has featured it since. In 1986 the XLH replaced the XLX Sportster, featuring the 883cc Evolution. This smaller displacement engine (V2) offers upgraded crankshaft components as well as improved cylinder heads, pistons, and a hydraulic lifter system. The traditional four-speed gearbox was retained.

Additional features of the Evolution included oval combustion chambers, computer-designed camshaft, three-piece flywheels, and improved intake-exhaust systems.

Two Evolution engine options currently prevail. The smaller is the 883cc V2 Evolution; the larger is the 1100cc version. Both provide superior oil flow and cooling, another area in which they excel over their Shovelhead predecessors (Fig. 1-10).

1-10
The new Sportster evolution motor. Two versions are marketed: an 883cc and a 1200cc.

Harley riders are a distinct and select breed. From the rich and famous down to everyday working-class individuals, they all share a common bond: a love and fascination for Harley-Davidson machines. It's hard to explain the appeal of a Harley to someone who has never experienced the "Harley Ride." The Harley buff experiences the true passion of motorcycling. The late Malcolm Forbes, who didn't start riding until the age of 50 and who collected over 50 brands and types of motorcycles from classics to race bikes, stated it perfectly in his book *More Than I Dreamed*: "Motorcycles are like racehorses. You want to have the best blood lines, and that means to have a Harley, if you can." The Harley is the most sought-after motorcycle in the world—not just here but in Japan, Europe, all around the globe.

The Japanese have manufactured many Harley look-alikes, but characteristically they differ from the unique Harley-Davidson cruisers. The sounds emanating from Japanese counterparts are akin to buzzing or warbling; some of them sound like hyperactive sewing machines. They shift gears silently; some consider this a plus, but not Harley folks. On a Harley you know you have shifted gears; you can feel and hear the throaty engine sound, the healthy BRRAAP when you start or accelerate the powerful V-twin engine. Japanese bikes all sound alike but you can always tell a Harley blindfolded by the distinct sound of its engine at rest or at speed. These characteristics as well as the riding comfort of the production Harley-Davidsons have endeared themselves to the bonafide Harley buff.

Harley-Davidson models & engines **9**

Harley-Davidson enthusiasts are strongly individualistic; they each want their bikes to have a look not similar to other riders. In the past they took their stockers and dressed them up with accessory goodies from aftermarket manufacturers (which still make a host of bolt-ons and add-ons for Harley buffs). One of the answers that new Harley management came up with was to work on the potential of a "factory custom" motorcycle. Based on this strategy, Harley built many customer-desirable custom refinements right into a variety of their factory models. Then they added an extensive line of custom accessories to allow owners to expand their customizing capabilities. Customers can add a host of specialized accessory goodies while allowing their machine to maintain the authentic "Harley" look that is desired.

The 1992 line of Harley-Davidson motorcycles encompasses 20 models in all. The newest model is the Dyna Glide custom, an upgraded version featuring developments inaugurated in the limited edition "Sturgis" and "Dyna Daytona" introduced in March of 1991. Also featured in the new Harley line are the Dyna Glide FXD series, the venerable Electra Glide FL, the FX and FL softail models, the FXR Low Riders and XL Sportsters (Figs. 1-11 through 1-15).

1-11
The XLH Sportster is the entry-level Harley motorcycle: low in price, high in quality.

1-12
FXRS Lowrider takes on the custom low look
currently popular in custom street cruisers.

1-13
The FXST Sprinter Softail features the new
softail frame with the hardtail look and a
Springer-type front fork.

1-14
The FXSTC Softail is the custom-styled softail featuring telescopic instead of springer-type front forks.

The newly-engineered Dyna chassis incorporated in the Dyna Customs features rubber-damped engine mounting to minimize engine vibrations and smooth the ride. Before the end of 1991, all Harley-Davidson models will be powder-coated (electrostatically painted), giving the machines hard, baked-on color coats. The revolutionary baked-on finish is a new high-tech paint system that Harley is pioneering—a worldwide first.

The 1992 models will also feature the powerful 80 c.i. 1340cc Evolution engines with new rejetted 40mm Mikuni carburetion.

The new carbs will offer improved cold starting and fuel delivery. Other features include steel oil lines, new oil pump mounting, the oil filter mounted in front of the engine for easier accessibility and maintenance, improved, highly efficient disk brake pad compounds, and improved belt-drive sprocket retainer. Chain-drive model Harleys starting in 1992 will all come equipped with O-ring chains.

What causes such enthusiasm about Harley-Davidsons? Harleys are coveted by men and women in all walks of life;

1-15
The Daytona (top) and Dyna Glide (bottom) are two of the newest Hot Harleys leading the 1992 lineup.

they share a common bond that equalizes all Harley owners. They love their Harleys.

The Harley-Davidson Motor Company is an example of the American success story; it exemplifies continuing American patriotism and product loyalty. The Harley-Davidson logo signifies "Quality Made in America." As stylish as Japanese cruiser counterparts may be, they are not Harley-Davidsons. They can emulate the look but never capture the essence, charisma, or quality that is essentially Harley-Davidson.

Frames & related components

THE FRAME is the structural foundation of every bike, integrating the rear swing arm or hardtail and front end, and also serving as the engine cradle. In this chapter we will cover frames and their related components, which together constitute the motorcycle's basic framework.

Many Harley enthusiasts find the hardtail frame most desirable on today's as well as yesterday's street machines. The new Harley Softail Evolution incorporates the hardtail look, but its special rear frame conceals a functional sprung softail version that gives the rider rear suspension (Fig. 2-1). Another frame suspension option is the swing arm (Fig. 2-2), which works in conjunction with shock absorbers in the rear end; some feel it gives the most comfortable ride. The choice is up to the rider.

Frame types

2-1
The new softail Harley rear suspension provides the hardtail look with the comfort of hidden shock absorber suspension.

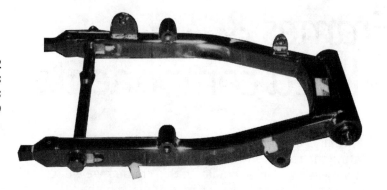

2-2
Swing arm suspension is another alternate. This custom unit was chromed to enhance appearance.

Those who opt for the rigid frame can be gratified in knowing that some fantastic aftermarket rigid frames are produced. Paughco, Inc., Carson City, Nevada, a leader in quality rigid-frame manufacturing, offers a host of hardtail frames for all Harley engines. More than 100 options are available with any rake configuration you might desire. By special order, specific custom raking is also available (Fig. 2-3).

2-3
Paughco custom frames are available for your custom bike.

Aftermarket frames such as the Paughco units are highly recommended for builders who want to fabricate from the ground up. All component parts will fit into the Paughco frame specifically designed for your particular model Harley. These frames offer tough billet steel mounts for engines and other components.

Handling

Handling characteristics of a bike are partially a matter of personal preference. Just as you choose between a hard or soft frame, you must decide whether you prefer a hard or soft ride. Since handling is relative to many aspects of frame plus suspension design, a specific machine might represent a compromise between the strongest frame and the lightest one, or between high-speed stability and low-speed cornering. Studying these factors of handling will help you make the best choices for your custom (Figs. 2-4 through 2-6).

2-4
Telescopic front forks provide good front suspension and offer excellent handling and cornering.

2-5
The Springer front end consolidates its suspension in the upper part of the front end and provides up-and-down damping via the wheel rockers, which work in unison with the springs.

2-6
Close-up view of the Springer damping springs. Springers are big in the cosmetics department.

Steering geometry

You've heard stories of motorcycles developing front-end wobble—oscillation that makes the forks tend to slap at either side of the gas tank. At the other extreme there is the tale of the dirt rider who is pitched off his saddle only to watch his machine propel itself onward, untended, for 100 feet or so. These examples show how a motorcycle's stability can be affected by the design of the front end. Most machines have their steering geometry set up so that the front wheel is pulled along by—or *trails*—the steering axis similar to the way a trailer follows behind a tow bar.

This self-aligning property in a motorcycle frame is usually achieved by inclining (or *raking*) the steering head around which the front fork pivots. Consequently, the central steering axis is tilted forward, striking the ground some distance ahead of the bike and leading the point where the front tire rests on the pavement by several inches. The distance between the intersection of the steering axis and the ground and midpoint of tire contact is called *trail*. The vertical angle at which the steering head is inclined is called the *caster angle* and is usually (but not always) the same as the rake angle. More on this later.

To measure the trail on your bike, simply take a string with a plumb bob or similar weight fastened to one end, then tape the other end to the front axle, allowing the weighted end to point downward to the center point of tire-to-ground contact. Then use a good straightedge to sight down along the steering neck to see where the imaginary axis hits the ground. Mark the point with chalk or a marker. To do this, you might need to remove the front wheel. The distance between the plumb line point and the chalk line point is the trail.

If you want a simpler, less tedious way to measure trail, photograph your bike directly from the side (at a 90-degree angle to the camera lens) with a ruler or yardstick alongside it for scale. Have the photo enlarged. You can easily mark the axis and tire tangent on the photograph.

It is possible to design frames with some trail and still have little or no steering and rake angle. Some antique bikes managed to handle well in such cases, but with the overall weights and high speeds attained on today's Harleys, some amount of rake is essential for good cornering and handling. A simple thing like parking and leaning a bike to the side will promote a turning effect in the forks. When rake and caster angle are correct, the forks will turn just the right amount to negotiate a turn as the motorcycle tilts when rounding that bend. In addition, raking the forks and steering head backward will prevent the front wheel from deflecting to the side when hitting a bump.

Rake is the amount of angle that the fork tubes are tilted from the vertical. *Caster* or *steering angle* is the degree of angle that the steering head has been displaced from the vertical. On most motorcycles, rake and caster angle will be the same since fork tubes are parallel to the steering neck (Fig. 2-7). Because the steering head is connected to the fork tubes via the triple clamps, an increase in steering head angle will also increase trail. As the front fork is tilted backward, the axis of steering slants ahead of the motorcycle (Fig. 2-8).

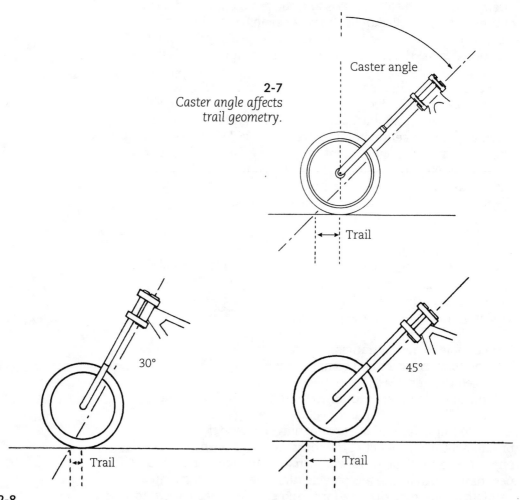

2-7
Caster angle affects trail geometry.

Caster angle

Trail

30°

Trail

45°

Trail

2-8
Increasing steering head angle will also increase trail. When the front fork tilts back the axis of steering slants ahead of the motorcycle.

Years ago—as far back as 1934—Harley-Davidson introduced what was then termed a special Desert Frame that contained a steering head raked a few degrees over normal, formulated on the sound idea that the increased rake and trail would allow more stable steering over the large bumps encountered in off-road riding. Somewhere along the way someone must have ridden the Desert Frame on a highway and discovered that more stable high-speed handling could also be realized on the pavement. Furthermore, on long trips at prolonged high speeds, a machine with a raked-out front end was less likely to skitter around, making it less tiring to ride. Soon after, bike owners accepted the principle and began to rake out their front ends by modifying their neck angles.

There are a number of accepted methods for increasing rake and trail. One of the early favored methods, which became very popular in the 1960s, was to cut, section, and reweld the frame tubes at the head of the frame. Up to that time, custom pre-raked frames were not available, so many rake jobs were home-brewed by certain individuals who either eyeballed the rake or built crude or elaborate jigs to assist them.

The procedure shown was done by Heaven on Wheels Custom Cycles & Accessories, Oakland Park, Florida (see Appendix for address). In Fig. 2-9, you can see a typical stock frame neck. An oxyacetylene cutting torch is used to make the V-cut. This gusset section must be cut out to allow for bending the neck tube. Heat is then applied to the top back frame tube until the joint is cherry red. Then a crowbar is inserted into the neck collar from the bottom, and while the steel is red hot and malleable, the collar is bent out until the desired rake angle is obtained.

After the proper neck angle has been achieved, gusset plates are cut to fit into the sides of the neck to fill in the area (Fig. 2-10). The new gusset plates are arc-welded into place to strengthen the reworked area (see Fig. 2-11 on page 24).

Raking stock or existing frames is not popular today and virtually all bike owners prefer to buy a custom-manufactured raked frame for several reasons. First, there are not many people qualified to do proper frame raking or knowledgeable in

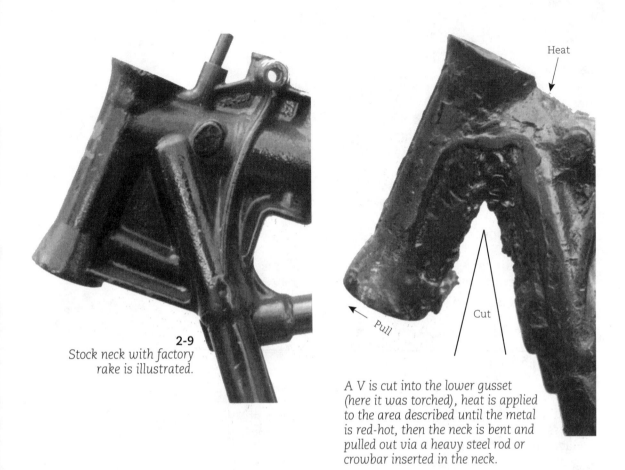

2-9
Stock neck with factory rake is illustrated.

Heat

Pull

Cut

A V is cut into the lower gusset (here it was torched), heat is applied to the area described until the metal is red-hot, then the neck is bent and pulled out via a heavy steel rod or crowbar inserted in the neck.

the welding and heating procedures involved. Excessive heat applied when welding and improper arc welding procedures tend to make metals brittle, particularly older frame metals. A weakened, improperly welded, or modified frame can be hazardous.

The new custom frames of today are fashioned of lighter chromemoly and similar alloys, which provide greater strength and lighter weight. In addition, they are exactingly constructed and are available made to order, incorporating any rake angle you desire. Custom factory-raked frames are the only way to go.

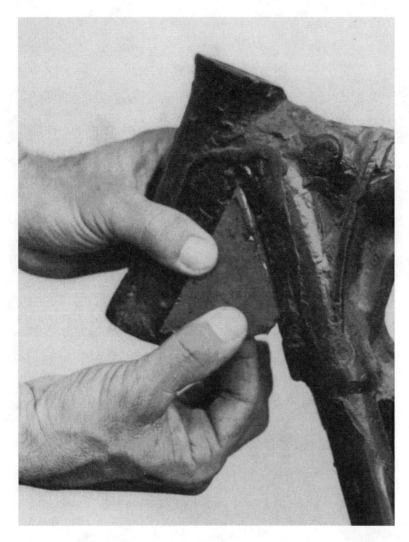

2-10
A new gusset is cut and fitted.

Another easier method used to increase rake is to install an extended front fork that raises the front end of the frame, pivoting around the rear wheel, effectively increasing the steering angle. More angle and backward tilt can be introduced into the frame as well by the use of a larger front wheel. For example, a 3.00×21-inch wheel will raise the front end 1½ inches over a 3.00×18-inch wheel.

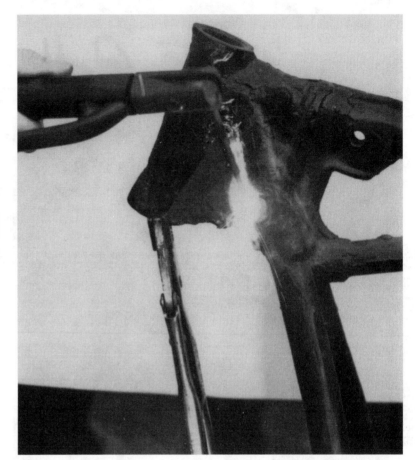

2-11
*The gusset is then welded
into place.*

Advantages of increased rake and trail at highway speeds must be weighed against some inherent shortcomings, however. Steering at slow speed tends to be heavy and the front wheel floppy. On sharp turns, the machine will understeer; steering response is slower, making curves feel sharper than they actually are. At extremely slow speeds, the self-aligning effect of trail will diminish with the forks tending to "flip flop" (fall to either side).

A motorcycle with a steeper fork and neck angle (and consequently less trail) will exhibit lighter, more responsive and more neutral steering, tending toward oversteer—and, in some cases, instability. The bike will react more rapidly to directional change.

The primary motive for extended front forks and rake angle is aesthetics. The amount of rake you incorporate into your frame or front end depends on how much handling and low-speed steering you want to sacrifice in the interest of looks. Many riders opt for a stock rake and basic look. Harley 74 c.i. models and the newer big bikes must cope with high speeds and dresser trim (saddlebags and so on) in the rear, which tend to lighten the front end, so they are designed with a stock rake of about 30 degrees and a trail slightly over four inches. Dragsters, on the other hand, for the conditions under which they are driven, require stable and predictable high-speed handling. Dragsters will exhibit rakes around the area of 40 degrees and trails up to eight inches.

Rake angles exceeding 10 degrees over stock can promote problems, since most original front suspensions are not made to function under radical back-tilt conditions. Telescopic forks are particularly prone to this problem, since the weight of the motorcycle places side load and drag on the bushings, inhibiting the fork sliders from sliding as easily as they would if the fork were in a position closer to vertical. When the front wheel hits a bump, the entire fork, tubes and all, tends to flex straight upward.

For more radical rakes, springer-type forks react more favorably, as the flexing rocker plates will allow more near-vertical wheel travel, regardless of the rake. A slight backward motion by the wheel is desirable, allowing the suspension to rebound from road irregularities more easily. If the line of wheel travel is parallel to the steering axis, there is almost no variation of trail as suspension travels up and down, which is desirable because steering geometry remains constant. Otherwise, steering will become alternately lighter and heavier as the bike traverses bumps and other road irregularities.

Extended forks are almost a must, therefore, when you realize that changing and kicking out the neck angle results in lowering the bike if stock-length forks are used. For this reason, fork tube extensions must be used in the case of telescopic forks or a custom-sized springer. Another alternative would be the use of a larger diameter front wheel. Extended forks are essential for raising a front end with or without a rake, and for leveling or retaining original frame clearance of a machine with a raked neck.

Contrary to popular opinion, a higher center of gravity will tend to make a motorcycle *more* stable at high speeds and less prone to the effects of crosswinds and road irregularities. A higher center of gravity will, on the other hand, require more effort and more control leaning in cornering. A high center of gravity also gives the bike a topheavy feel at low speeds. Extra-long forks will tend to flex and bend, making the front tire want to tilt and turn of its own accord. This can promote some premature steering effects that you might not count on or want. On telescopic forks, this effect can be minimized or remedied by adding a fork brace. Springers are less prone to fork flexing because of their inherent, restricted suspension movements.

Wheelbase

Wheelbase should also be considered a handling factor, because it is relative to the effects of rake, trail, and center of gravity. Raking the neck and extending the front end also increases the wheelbase. Wheelbase may also be extended by lengthening the rear of a hardtail frame or the rear swing arm of a sprung frame. A long wheelbase increases stability at the cost of a greater turning radius and slower handling.

In essence, the properties of a longer wheelbase reinforce the characteristics of added rake and trail and high center of gravity. The longest wheelbase on a factory Harley-Davidson was 60 inches on the Harley 74 c.i. How much stretch you implement between the wheels is a matter of personal preference, but stretching the wheelbase beyond 72 inches will probably make your custom extremely difficult to maneuver and jockey around.

Once you have completed the raking and extending procedures, you might find that even though you have done everything necessary to achieve your expectations, you wind up with low-speed handling a bit on the heavy side—a bit too heavy for your liking, anyway. All is not lost, however. You can implement a few tricks to reduce trail and steering angle without reraking the neck and still retain your extended front-end look.

If you are installing a springer front end, you can use or have made extra-long rocker plates that will locate the front wheel closer to the steering axis and reduce trail to a reasonable amount. Some ready-made springers manufactured today incorporate this feature into their offerings. The lengths of the links on girder forks can be changed to rake out the girder, moving the wheel forward and diminishing trail. The important factor in these cases is never to reduce trail to zero, and *never* let the point of tire contact get forward of the steering axis where the tire strikes the ground (Fig. 2-12).

If the front fork angle alone is altered without raking the steering head, the amount of trail will shrink very quickly and its stabilizing and self-aligning effects will also diminish. Bikes with little or no trail or minus trail are ridable, since there are other stabilizing factors (such as rib design on tires) that assist wheels in running straight. The gyroscopic effect of the bike wheels also helps stabilize them as they spin faster. Reduced trail is not recommended, however, if you like to do a lot of comfortable riding.

2-12
Rake, trail, and caster angle geometry as applied to the springer front end.

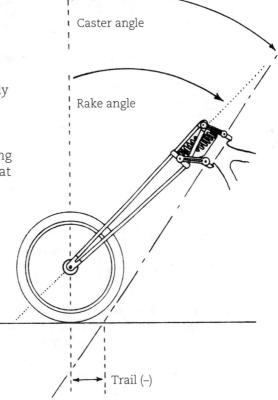

Caster angle

Rake angle

Trail (–)

Frames & rigidity

There are pros and cons as to which is better, a rigid or a spring frame. There is only one discriminating factor here, and it has been exercised ever since bikers began customizing and modifying. That factor is *personal choice*. A desired prerequisite for good handling is a strong, flex-free frame that situates front and rear wheels in proper positions so that they do not skew and swivel, pounding over bumps under cornering pressure. Although rigid rear frame sections give a hard ride and tend to bounce, they provide excellent handling on smoother terrain. With their inherent triangular shape, they are relatively free of torsional stresses that often cause rear swing arms to work independently, causing possible adverse wheel tilt at the wrong moment.

Modified bikes—choppers in particular—place more than normal stress on the steering head and front downtubes. For this reason you see a lot of kicked-out front necks with gussets or side plates, and "molding in," which through enhancing the bike's appearance serves to strengthen the neck area, which probably receives most of the stress applied to a frame. Remember, a good, reinforced rigid frame will do much to reduce frame oscillation and wheel wobble.

If optimum riding comfort is your bag, a sprung or swing-arm rear end might be the way to go. In many instances, a sprung rear wheel can work better to keep your bike on track if it can maintain contact with the ground most of the time, handling bumps and irregularities more smoothly. A swing arm must also incorporate vertical rigidity, or the individual arms can try to flex separately instead of staying in alignment. But this is no problem with Harley swing arms and the newer Softail models. The Softail Harley frames not only provide sound rear suspension, but also give the hardtail frame a triangular rear-end look that is very fashionable on today's Harley Low Riders.

Front forks

Front forks also aid in providing a smoother ride for both rigid and sprung frames. Front-end suspension will also reduce frame stress by absorbing jolts and bumps. In the event that your front-end springing is too soft or hard, you can make modifications to balance with rear-end suspension. The springs on a front end are often wound in a two-rate or progressive manner; the farther they are compressed, the stiffer they become. The springing can be stiffened by altering the pitch of the spring winding (crowding more coils into the same spring length), such as the long spring inside glide tubes. Another method is changing the actual diameter of the coil winding, such as the barrel spring in the center of many early girder forks. Stiffer or softer replacement springs can be obtained for glide or springer front ends, if required.

Damping

Friction damping with dual circular pads that rotated against each other was utilized in many girder front forks. These had the advantage of being adjustable. By tightening down on the two disks by means of a threaded knob, you could increase friction and damping. But any damping that was applied in this method worked equally in compression and rebound, with the possibility of a ride that was either too stiff on the way down or too harsh on the way up. Most sophisticated damping today is via the hydraulic method, by squeezing oil through a series of holes or passages, which serves to soak up the force of a bump.

Oil damping can be designed to offer a variety of absorption rates on compression or rebound. Most of today's hydraulic damping systems prevail only on telescopic front-fork systems, but some recently designed springers incorporate both spring and hydraulic units. These would affect the advantages of telescoping forks, which would be optimum damping, with the aesthetic custom look of springers.

The final choice of looks versus roadability is up to you. If you want your bike to be a radical showpiece, you must live with some of the maneuverability shortcomings. If the machine will be used for functional transportation, you might want to be a bit conservative and incorporate some low-speed handling advantages.

If you opt for sprung suspension and ride, I suggest you leave it as close to stock as possible. If the hardtail frame, ride, and look is your choice, I recommend a Paughco custom frame, which is lighter than a stock Harley unit and will accommodate any year Harley engine. Of course, you must specify year and model so you can obtain the frame unit tailored to your Harley.

In the 1960s, hardtail add-on units were in vogue and obtainable in two versions: bolt-on (bolting on to Harley frame sections with deleted swing arms) and weld-on. Both have fallen out of grace, primarily for safety reasons. The bolt-on versions tended to work loose due to frame and engine vibration. (It was almost impossible to keep the nuts and bolts from working loose.) The welded-on units tended to make the adjoining stock frame sections brittle, and under the hard riding conditions a hardtail was subjected to, they could break off, especially if a qualified welder did not undertake the joining procedure correctly.

Frame aesthetics

At best, Harley-Davidson frames are a compromise, built to operate functionally with some regard for looks. On the average street machine, with tanks, fenders, engines and so on, the aesthetic shortcomings are for the most part hidden or not noticeable unless scrutinized. Under such scrutiny, however, flaws such as reinforcement ribs, gusset plates, and unsightly welds do tend to detract from a bike, especially if it is custom-finished and painted.

It is common and fashionable to upgrade the looks of the street machine and modified bike by molding the frame. In the case of show customs, it is a prerequisite and highly essential. Within the following pages, we'll look at how this is done and the techniques applicable to molding in a Harley-Davidson or aftermarket accessory frame.

Plating & gusseting

I took a personal approach in modifying the Paughco frame shown (Fig. 2-3). Not only was the frame molded, but it was also modified to finish off the neck, fill in the seat area with fill-in plating and molding, and add a decorative perforated gusset fill-in plate between the front downtubes—personal touches that make the frame more distinctive.

The plating and welding were undertaken by Red Racing, a custom car and motorcycle facility in Boca Raton, Florida, specializing in definitive custom and structural work. The welding was done by Red Racing's ace resident welder, Scott Christie, one of the best in the business.

Molding and finishing the neck is one of the most important facets of beautifying your frame. On this particular frame, an aftermarket offering by Paughco, the plates are an integral part of the frame, an added plus found in all the Paughco offerings. If a stock Harley frame is utilized, the plates also must be fashioned, cut, and welded on (Fig. 2-13).

The next phase involved fashioning the gusset plate for the front end. First, a template was made (Fig. 2-14) by tracing the area between the front downtubes onto a piece of paper or heavy cardboard. The tracing need not be exact, but it is better to make the pattern oversized rather than undersized, as it can be trimmed down and sized to fit after the pattern is cut from the board.

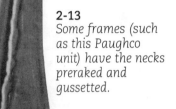

2-13
Some frames (such as this Paughco unit) have the necks preraked and gussetted.

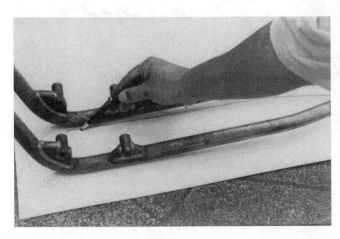

2-14
A tracing is made between the front fork legs in order to size the fill-in plating section.

After cutting, the template is laid in place (Fig. 2-15). A centerline is then drawn vertically to help situate the hole pattern on the template, and holes are laid out using a

2-15
The template is critically sized after putting it into place.

compass (Fig. 2-16). When the template pattern is finished, it is cut out and traced onto a piece of sheet steel. I chose ³⁄₃₂-inch thick plate, but ⅛-inch steel will suffice for this operation. Steel thinner than ⅛-inch will tend to warp when welded.

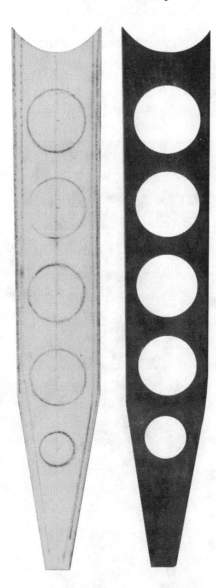

2-16
At left is the template; at right, the plate cut and ready for installation in the frame.

To cut the plate, a steel-cutting bandsaw was utilized, carefully cutting the steel along the specified guideline (Figs. 2-17, 2-18) and tack welded (arc-welded) into place (Fig. 2-19). Stitch welding is recommended at spaced intervals, as arc-welding a bead down the entire length of the tubes would tend to weaken and embrittle the tube metal, which could cause it to crack under riding stress. Stitch welding will more than secure the plate, which is a decorative rather than structural part to begin with. The intermediate spaces can then be filled in with brass by brazing and then filling (Fig. 2-20). Welds are then ground down and the joints smoothed off (Figs. 2-21, 2-22).

2-17
A band saw is utilized for the fine curved cuts.

2-18
A hole saw inserted into a drill press serves to cut out the plate openings.

2-19
The plate is tack-welded into place for alignment by "stitching" with the electric welder.

2-20
Edges are "frenched"; brazed in.

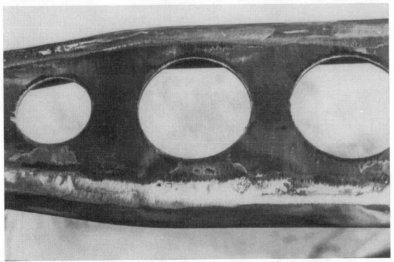

In Fig. 2-23, you can also study the front decorative gusset plate in place with the metalwork finished. To further enhance the overall streamlined look of the bike, I chose to fill in the seat framework section (Fig. 2-24). Templates were cut from cardboard, then transferred to sheet metal in the same manner as the larger plate. The cutout steel fillers were then arc-welded into place.

2-23
The completed frame ready for filler.

2-24
The seat section was also gussetted to improve and refine the frame's appearance.

Later on in this chapter I will show how the frame is further refined and contoured with the aid of plastic body filler (Figs. 2-25, 2-26).

2-25
Rear view of the custom frame
shows the modified front section and seat section.

2-26
Here's an approach (by Heaven-on-Wheels) where the seat section is filled in, bordered with the rear fender welded into the seat section and braced on the hardtail piece.

Frames & related components 39

Molding is the fine-finishing aspect of custom frame modification. Once all the groundwork such as plating and gusseting is finished, it is the easiest but most time-consuming part of the job if the frame is to be flawlessly finished.

Molding-in the frame

Before applying body fillers, the metal on the frame must be scrupulously clean—free from rust, dirt, grime and so forth. This will allow the filler to adhere positively to the metal surface. Welds should be ground down and cleaned off (Fig. 2-27). A wire brush in a drill or air grinder will access all the crevices (Fig. 2-28). It is highly recommended that the frame be sandblasted after the metalwork is completed. You can rent a small air-powered hand blaster that will do the job quickly and efficiently for about $20 to $30.

2-27
Metal sections to be filled in are prepped—sanded clean or wire-brushed—to remove rust and dirt so that the filler will adhere.

2-28
The wire brush gets into all the nooks and crannies.

For starters it is wise to grind down all the welds, particularly in all the small corners, cross-tube areas, motor mounts, and the tail ends. A small, one-inch Carborundum grinder in a drill or air driver works best in these areas. The more you can finish-grind the weld beading, the less filler you will have to apply—which is preferable, since you want to keep your plastic filleting to a minimum (Fig. 2-29). The work will be time-consuming, but necessary.

2-29
Welds can be ground down with a "lollipop" grinder, which gets into the confined spots.

Plastic filling is the final stage of molding-in, and there are many plastic fillers available such as Bondo, Duraglass, and metal-impregnated fillers. Many customers choose automotive body filler such as Bondo. Bondo is easy to work and sands well without too much hassle. It is, however, too porous for my liking and seems a bit more prone to cracking. Metal-impregnated fillers such as Alum-a-Lead and All-Metal are very strong but are hard to work and fine finish when they have fully hardened. With the time involved in fine finishing, sanding, and contouring a frame, a greater part of the filler will fully harden. Therefore, the best compromise for me is Duraglass.

Duraglass is a plastic filler impregnated with fiberglass for added strength. It is strong, less prone to cracking, and although not as easy to trim as Bondo, will sand and file down quite easily. Duraglass, like other body fillers, is a two-part medium that must be catalyzed prior to use to promote chemical hardening of the filler. The filler is mixed according to the directions on the can and when filler and hardener are properly mixed (blended), the filler is applied over the area to be molded with a squeegee (Fig. 2-30).

2-30
Filler is mixed then applied with a squeegee as shown.

The filler should be applied liberally—that is, enough to cover the area but not excessively so that you distort the contour of the metal. In about 10 minutes the material can be shaved and sanded. Plastic body files are used to rough-shave body fillers just as they set but before they harden. On neck areas the files do not work as well, as it is hard to work around the neck contours with them. They are more beneficial for use in larger, flatter areas. I like to use sandpaper and sanding blocks to finish off neck areas, as many professional molders do (Fig. 2-31). To work in tight areas around the neck tube, a tapered round file or rasp is essential (Fig. 2-32).

2-31
Filler is sanded and contoured with a sanding block.

2-32
A round file works the filler in the tight corners.

In the photograph, a skim coat of filler was applied around the front plate welds to fill in flaws and imperfections. Then the plate area was finished off with an 80-grit sanding disk and holder powered by an electric drill. A dual orbital air sander will do the job as well (Fig. 2-33).

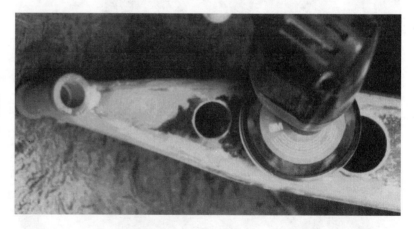

2-33
A disk sander contours and refines the plate.

Next, the seat area is filled in in the same manner as the neck to gap and layer the seat plating (Fig. 2-34).

2-34
Filler is applied to the molded seat gusset.

Since the seat area is flatter and more accessible, a body file was used to shape and work the Duraglass. The body file should be implemented immediately after the filler has set and prior to hardening. This will allow the filler to be easily shaved, cut down, and shaped. The softer the filler, the easier it shaves down (Fig. 2-35). Once it has hardened after contouring, the Duraglass can be finely contoured with a sanding block, which will aid in attaining smooth, straight surface areas (Fig. 2-36).

2-35
A cheese grater file is used to contour the plated area.

Frames & related components 45

2-36
Block-sanding finishes off the procedure.

Coarse sandpaper such as 36-grit is great for cutting down Duraglass quickly with less sanding effort. However, it leaves some mean-looking scratches.

For final smoothing, I advise using 80-grit sandpaper after the rough work has been done using 36-grit. Occasionally, either to build up the molding or to fill in irregularities that can appear in a first or inappropriate coat of filler, it is necessary to put on additional coats, or, in the case of minor irregularities, a skim coat of filler. It is wise to blow away the surface after initial finishing in order to bare some of the irregularities (Fig. 2-37).

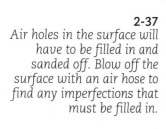

2-37
Air holes in the surface will have to be filled in and sanded off. Blow off the surface with an air hose to find any imperfections that must be filled in.

Another tip: When sanding curves in filled areas such as the gradual curve in the seat plate being molded, sandpaper wrapped around a tube will make the job easier while maintaining the curve, whereas the block serves more efficiently for level sanding (Fig. 2-38).

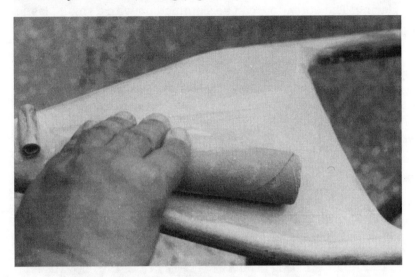

2-38
Sandpaper wrapped around a dowel or tube helps in curved contouring.

Once you have achieved a flawless surface, you can prime the area for added filling and to bring out any minor imperfections such as nicks or scratches (Fig. 2-39).

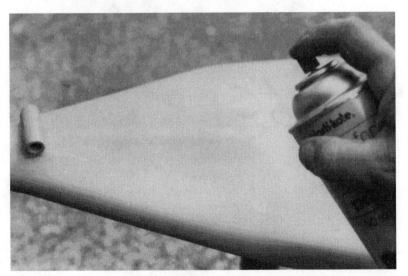

2-39
Prime the area to fill in minor imperfections.

Frames & related components 47

If surface blemishes do occur (and they usually do the first or second time around), they can be filled in with NitroStan body putty, a glazing medium designed to fill in minor nicks and scratches. NitroStan can only be applied over a primed surface, as it doesn't bond well to filler, so you must prime prior to glazing. The putty, too, can be skimmed on with a small plastic or rubber squeegee (Fig. 2-40). The putty should be given a few hours to air-dry, then must be fine-sanded with 220-grit sandpaper.

2-40
If nicks and chips and scratches show through the primer, skim-coat some glazing putty on and resand until scratches are leveled off.

After sanding and making sure you have a perfect surface, you can prime and paint over it. If you wish to cut down your glazing dry time, I can recommend Evercoat catalyzed glazing putty (Fig. 2-41). Evercoat is a two-part solution mixed in the same fashion as plastic filler, but the catalyzing action allows it to fully dry in minutes so that your fine sanding can commence almost immediately after applying putty. Nicks and blemishes will greatly benefit from topcoat glazing, which will make the blemishes disappear after final sanding (Fig. 2-42).

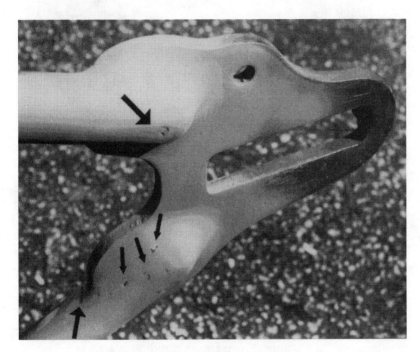

2-41
Arrows point out the kind of surface imperfections that manifest themselves.

The hardest parts to mold-in due to their tight access spaces are the rear frame mounts and brake retainer (Fig. 2-43). It is wise to file the welds down as much as possible in these areas, filling in with skim coats of body plastic. Sanding and contouring will have to be done with rat-tail files and contour files to negotiate all the protuberances.

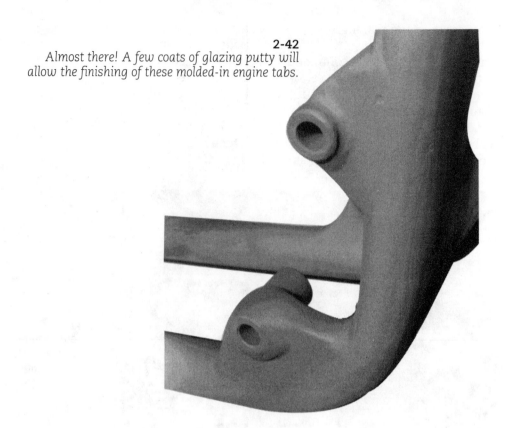

2-42
Almost there! A few coats of glazing putty will allow the finishing of these molded-in engine tabs.

A good overall glazing coat was also applied to the front gusset plate to fill in surface irregularities, particularly around the weld seams (Figs. 2-44, 2-45).

Some words of wisdom: Since frame molding is a time-consuming and lengthy process, it is helpful to do it one section at a time. For instance, the neck can be one operation, the seat area another, and so on. Finish each section fully; otherwise, lengthy intervals between operations can promote rusting of the frame in or around the areas you have worked, which will mean resanding and cleaning. Spot-prime all finished areas as you go along. You can use spray-can primers for the small areas involved in bike frames. This will protect the steel areas adjoining the filler areas from rust.

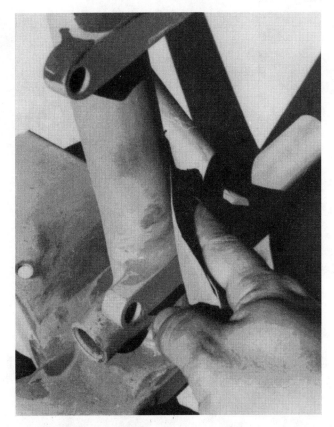

2-43
The rear down tube is filled and smoothed in.

2-44
Glazing putty over primer finishes off the front gusset plate.

Another recommendation is that after moldwork is completed, give the frame an overall spray coating of Feather Fill. Feather Fill is a catalyzed primer that goes on heavy and has the property of filling in dents and scratches you might have missed. After sanding down the Feather Fill, if all molding procedures have been followed as specified, you will have a flawless molding job (Figs. 2-46 through 2-49).

2-46
Here's another molded seat section piece by Heaven-on-Wheels on a Paughco frame.

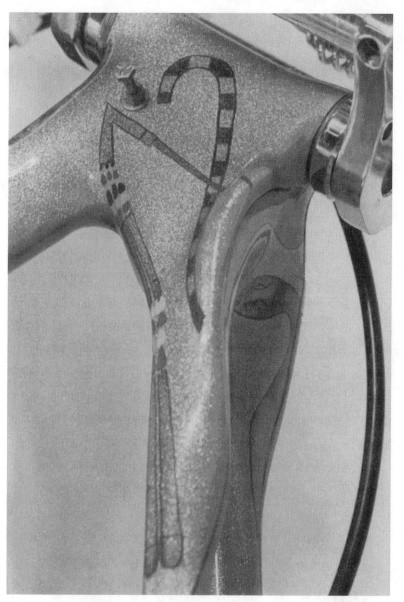

2-47
*Here's some fine molding by
John Lasky on a custom
Harley front down tube
section.*

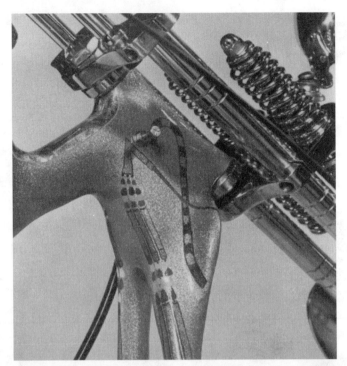

2-48
Rear view of the neck and down tube artistry of John Lasky.

2-49
Bobby Izzo's Right On sports some exquisite frame molding enhancement.

After painting and molding, the front end will serve as a decorative, eye-catching feature as well as a practical part of the frame.

The selection and application of a front end, be it stock or modified, should be carefully considered using the handling guidelines discussed earlier in this chapter. You must also consider the looks-versus-operation options and apply them to your tastes and needs. Many riders will choose to stay with their stock front ends, utilizing the telescopic tube and glide systems and coordinating them with a stretched neck rake by installing extended fork tubes, which easily replace stock tubes in a simple swap assembly operation (Fig. 2-50). Owners can have extended fork tubes installed by a Harley dealer, or can install them themselves following the fork assembly procedures spelled out in the Harley-Davidson shop manual. Extended fork tubes for big Glides, FLS and FXWG, Sportster FX, L, FXRT and FLH models can be obtained from such sources as Forking by Frank, Inc., Evanston, Illinois; CCI, Morgan Hill, California; and Nostalgia Cycle in Huntington Beach, California. Custom Chrome and Drag Specialties, Eden Prairie, Minnesota, also offer extended tube services. (See Appendix for supplier addresses.)

2-50
Forks (telescopic) can be extended by replacing stock tubes with accessory extra-length tubes from such sources as Forking by Frank.

The springer, another front-end offering dating in concept to the earlier Harleys, offers great appearance as well as performance features. There are several aftermarket accessory springers marketed that are excellent (Fig. 2-51).

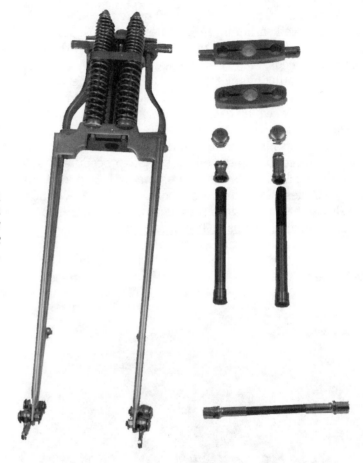

2-51
A fine springer with length options is marketed by Paughco; it's adaptable to all Harley frames.

In the 1970s, a number of accessory manufacturers produced springers. Many of those companies are now defunct, but every once in a while their products turn up in Harley shops or in swap meets. Today, springers can be purchased through Harley-Davidson dealerships, or from such sources as Finch's Custom Styled Cycles, Pontiac, Michigan, and Paughco, Inc.

Show customs usually feature modified and revamped springers in configurations from mild to wild.

Fenders & tanks

FENDERS & TANKS are functional components of a bike, but they also provide opportunities for customizing and embellishment with paint, sculptured effects, and molding.

There are a host of fender types—both stock or aftermarket modified—that will bolt on to Harley-Davidson motorcycles. The builder has the option to choose or modify them to his or her own individual taste.

Aftermarket or custom fenders are quite popular, as they are often lighter and more stylish—very applicable to trimming out a street machine or chopper. Fenders are marketed in both metal and fiberglass (for weight reduction), even contoured and sculptured (Fig. 3-1). Some are simple bolt-on replacements; others, such as the flat steel low-profile units, require special mounting (Fig. 3-2). Replacement or custom fenders are available from such sources as Custom Chrome, Inc. (CCI), Drag Specialties, and Paughco, Inc. (Fig. 3-4).

Fenders

3-1
Some uniquely sculptured fenders can be found, such as this fiberglass custom by Frenchies Novelty Fenders, available from Brothers III. Offerings like these are truly distinctive.

3-2
Shown here are two fiberglass aftermarket fenders by Drag Specialties. On the left is the Quickbob front fender for 1949–89 FL, FLH, FLHT, and FLT Harleys; on the right is the Quickbob for 1980–86 FXWGs and 1984–89 FXSTs.

Fenders can be glamorized by sculpturing or "bobbing," as you will see in this chapter, or they can be custom-painted with decorative motifs that will enhance their aesthetic value (Figs. 3-3, 3-5). In many instances, they can simply be painted in one color to match other painted segments of the bike.

3-3
I painted this fender for a show-custom Shovelhead. The interwoven ribbon motif is eye-catching. The fender is a replacement front by Drag Specialties designed for FX, FXR, and XL Harleys.

3-4
A trim steel fender for 1949–84 FLs with integrated chrome mounting bracket. The fender profile is designed to clear 18, 19, and 21-inch tires. Fender is by CCI.

3-5
Here's an example of tasteful op-art paneling on a modified Triumph fender. Modernistic artwork is by customizer Ron Finch of Pontiac, Michigan, a premier custom painter and bike builder.

Bobbing

Fender bobbing became popular among bike customizers in the 1960s and 1970s, particularly on choppers. Some bobbing or cutting back is still done, especially on street and show customs for the sake of creative styling.

The first step in cutting and trimming a fender is to determine the shortening length. Once determined, a band saw is used, whether the cut is to be straight across or fancy (Fig. 3-6). In this example, we are scalloping the end of a Harley modified rear fender. After cutting the scallop contours, we proceed to lip the scalloping to add both rigidity and to improve aesthetics.

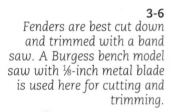

3-6
Fenders are best cut down and trimmed with a band saw. A Burgess bench model saw with ⅛-inch metal blade is used here for cutting and trimming.

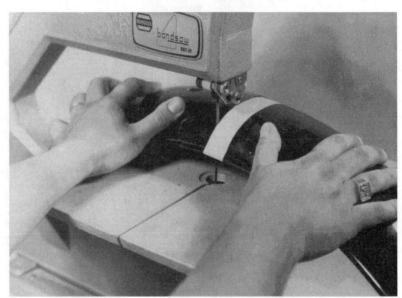

Either ¼-inch or ⅜-inch thick steel rod is excellent for this, and we attach it to the scalloped lips with the aid of a torch and brass brazing rod. The torch (oxyacetylene) heats the rod red-hot so that it can be bent and contoured to the scalloping while it is brass brazed (Fig. 3-7). After the rod is brazed into place, a grinder is used to grind away the excess brass and contour the lip evenly all around (Fig. 3-8). Small nicks and surface imperfections can be fine finished with plastic body filler, then sanded to perfection. The finished scalloped fender is then primed and ready to paint (Fig. 3-9).

3-7
The edge of the scalloping is beaded using ¼-inch thick rod formed and brazed on with an oxyacetylene torch with a fine brazing tip.

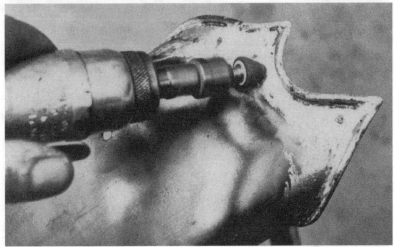

3-8
Excess brass is ground down with a die-grinder. A cone-shaped grinding bit allows access to confined areas. Minute nicks and grind marks are then filled in with skim coats of filler and sanded smooth.

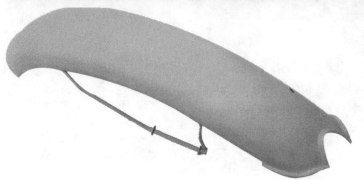

3-9
Here's the finished scalloped fender. This fender modification is truly eye-catching and unique.

Sculpturing

Sculptured fenders can be eye-catching and artistic and do much to enhance the overall appearance of a Harley, especially a show bike. First the pattern or contour lines for the fender end are drawn onto the steel with a grease pencil (Fig. 3-10). The contours are then rough-cut with a band saw using a ⅛-inch blade, fine-toothed for metal cutting. Woodcutting blades are not recommended for this procedure, as they do not have the tensile strength of metal band saw blades (Fig. 3-11). A grinder or Dremel hand motor tool is then implemented to fine finish and perfectly contour the edges (Fig. 3-12).

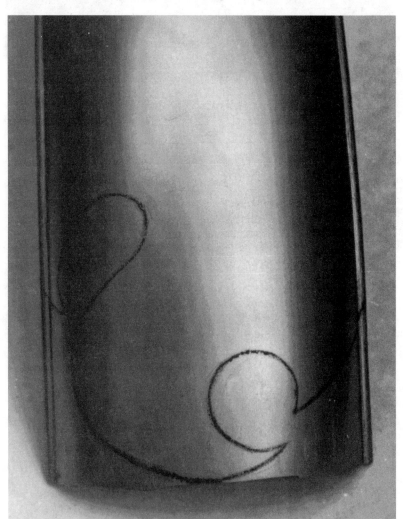

3-10
Prior to cutting the fender, the cutout design is drawn onto the surface. The cleaner and more precise the outlining, the easier it is to achieve an exacting cut with the band saw blade.

3-11
Prior to fine-cutting, access holes are cut out to enable the blade to swing around the small radii. Cut small sections at a time to ensure exactness.

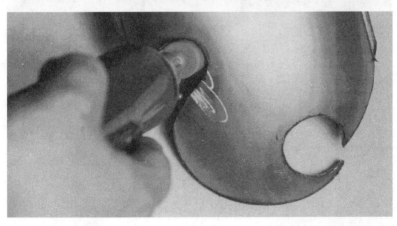

3-12
A die-grinder and round grinding "lollipop" is used to fine-finish the curves and cut edges. Time and patience applied here are crucial to obtain fine, exacting curves.

Next, a raised, contoured, waved center rib running the length of the fender is sculptured. A ⅛-inch rod is used to form the freeform contour rib, brazed in place, and tack-welded in the segments of the wire that touch the fender surface (Fig. 3-13). Some sections of the rod waves are raised off the surface to give more sculptural dimension to the rib. Intermediate areas are then filled in with plastic body putty and fine contoured by sanding with 80-grit sandpaper (Fig. 3-14).

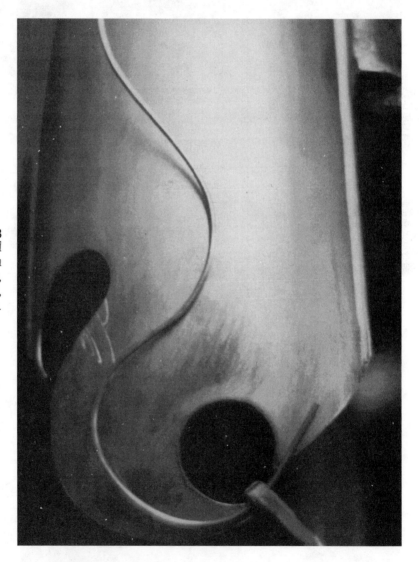

3-13
A preformed wire or rod stock (steel) is used to form the sculptured pattern. Here, steel welding rod was used, brazed on with brass.

3-14
Finished contouring is accomplished with plastic body filler. Final sanding and shaping is done with 80-grit sandpaper.

There are innumerable possibilities for creative sculptured effects using this simple method. Metal overlays can also be cut, inserted, and molded into fenders employing modern, freeform designs (Fig. 3-15).

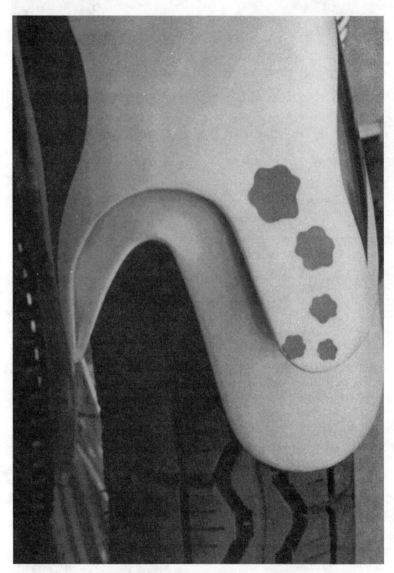

A number of tanks—stock issue, aftermarket replacement, and custom—are readily available from such sources as Paughco, Inc., CCI, and Drag Specialties. At one time during the 1970s, the heyday of the chopper, peanut tanks and Sportster tanks dominated, either out-of-the-box or modified (Fig. 3-16).

3-16
Here's another distinctive creation from Finch's Custom Styled Cycles. The side panels were formed by heating and indenting ovals into a peanut chopper tank with a ball hammer. Final finishing was achieved with filler sanded smooth. The oval was first outlined with steel rod. Paintwork is also by Ron Finch.

Today, they are still used but in stock specifications, as in the case of the Sportster tanks, with the peanut making a lesser appearance (Fig. 3-17). The hot setup on Harley-Davidsons today is the twin or one-piece "fat bob" tanks. Most street riders favor these tanks for their handsome profile and their gas efficiency (Fig. 3-18).

You must be careful when purchasing aftermarket tanks, however, since some inferior ones will tend to leak around the wells. Stick to Harley issue or acknowledged brands such as Paughco, both noted for their quality.

Customizing tanks for dimensional sculptured effect is similar to sculpturing fenders. Sheet steel and brass brazing rod is utilized to do the basic structural work, using the same methods spelled out in the fender-bob procedures (Fig. 3-19).

Tank molding & sculpturing

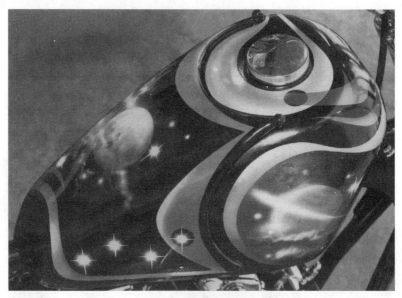

3-17
I created this example of sculpture overlay using the prescribed methods. The pattern was preformed with ⅜-inch thick steel rod, then sheathed in fine-gauge metal, brazed. It adds contour to the Sportster tank.

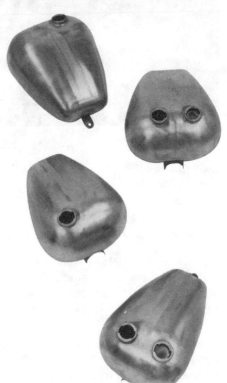

3-18
Classic aftermarket tanks are offered that enhance the overall styling of stock or show machines. These fat-bob replacement tanks by Paughco come in various one-piece versions and will mount to virtually all Harley frames with or without slight modification.

Tanks are also molded into frames, a show-custom technique that refines the overall looks of a bike, allowing the lines of the tank and frame to flow into each other, so to speak. In this procedure, the tank tabs are usually welded to the frame and the adjacent prominent areas are plated or filled in with $\frac{1}{16}$-inch or $\frac{1}{8}$-inch thick sheet steel cut to the proper fill-in dimensions (Fig. 3-20). Then the molding work is fine finished using auto body plastic filler.

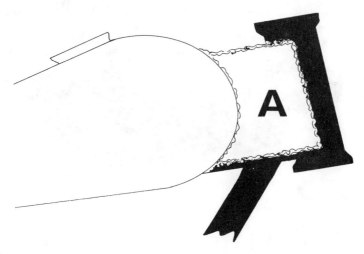

A

3-20
*A hypothetical situation
for molding a tank into a
frame. The precut plate (A)
is brazed, spanning the gap
between the frame and the
tank. Other spaces around
the tank can also be filled in
with brazed-in sheet steel.*

There is no end to what can be done to modify and enhance a tank's physical appearance. A little ingenuity can go a long way in creating highly decorative and artistic tank work (Figs. 3-21 through 3-23).

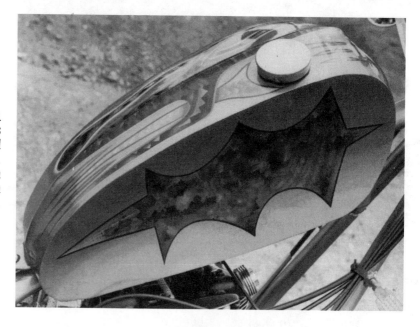

3-21
Talk about wild! This Triumph tank was sectioned and revamped by Ron Finch. Side panels were cut, then swapped, resulting in an ultra-distinctive look.

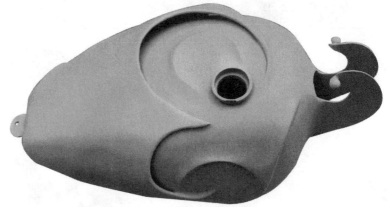

3-22
Here is another example of unique overlay sculpturing. The tank is a basic peanut chopper tank. Fine sculpture and metalwork is by Mardo Bennett, another great custom bike builder.

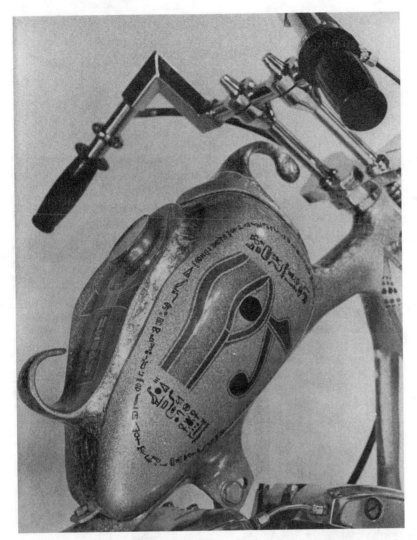

This magnificent example of classic sculpture is on Nile Style (officially named Scepter of Egypt), a prominent show custom dating to the mid-1970s. Sculpture and paintwork are by John Lasky.

Bodywork

In the custom motorcycle world, paneling and molding are commonly instituted to conceal unsightly brackets, welds, and forging marks. Sheet metal can be used to radius or fill in sharp corners for additional cosmetic effects. In some cases it can also have a functional use; switch panels or gauges can be mounted in the metal. A blending of metal might connect with and strengthen a rear strut, fender, or other structural component of a bike (Figs. 3-24 and 3-25). The three basic requirements for

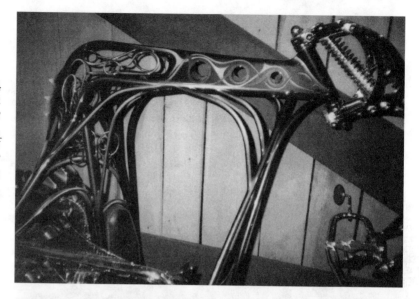

3-24
The metal-filling work can be seen in this trike frame by Ron Finch. Good bracing, coupled with the use of ⅛-inch steel plate, makes for a strong frame and neck structure.

3-25
More distinctive sheetmetal work by Finch, this time on a new Evolution frame wildly modified. Classic op-art sculpture is evidenced here.

high-quality bodywork are using the right material, in the right thickness, and the correct method of connection. Brass welding is the acknowledged fastening method for custom sculpture work and Frenching on steel frames and parts. On alloy tanks and fenders, the work should be done with heliarc welding and aluminum. For relatively minor work and finishing, the builder can rely on the plastic body fillers currently on the market. Body fillers can be utilized to fill in small, rough spots and smoothen ridges. For major, large-area work it is preferable to span or fill with sheet metal. The rule of thumb varies, but usually anything that requires more than a ⅜-inch thickness of body filler should be done in metal.

I'm sure there are many one- and two-inch Bondo jobs that have held up through the years; on the other hand, I know that discerning custom builders limit their thicknesses of filler to ⅛ inch. Some don't even use fillers, preferring to fill with brass and then grind it down. Part of this decision depends on the structural piece underneath. If it is a stout frame tube, a heavy layer of filler can be applied without cracking. A thin, flimsy fender will not take as much.

Proper metal thickness must be considered and is usually decided upon depending on the size or distance being spanned by the sheet metal. A small cleanup of the seat post area where the supporting frame tubes are fairly close together would probably work well in 18 or 22 gauge steel. Stretching a panel across the two legs of a hardtail would require something much thicker because of the span involved and the fact that the panel is not supported on the third side. To play it safe, ⅛-inch or 10 gauge steel would be better for this type of application.

Mounting fenders

The appearance of a bike can also be enhanced by using the varied accessory fenders supplied by many custom accessory outlets. These are easy to mount using basic bolt-on procedures.

Typical are the flat fenders, which do much to slim down the overall lines of a machine—much desired in bikes styled along chopper lines. The flat fender is a universal-type unit and must be custom mounted; it is not a predrilled, bolt-on unit. Other flat or narrow fenders are also marketed along the same lines for both front and rear applications. Front chopper fenders usually come with accommodating brackets that will conform to Harley front-fender fork mountings, but the rear fenders, such as shown here, need a little fitting and sizing. Many stock Harley fenders are interchangeable (as well as custom replacement fenders), and sometimes the swapping and interchanging of these fenders on various makes of Harley will provide some basic styling changes.

To properly mount the fender, you must first mount the wheel in its proper position. The fender must be mounted so that it follows the curve of the wheel precisely, ensuring the correct distance between the tread and fender well. I find that a simple way to do this is to lay a folded towel, layered to allow ½ to ¾ inch between tread and fender wall, over the tire as shown in Fig. 3-26.

3-26
A folded towel is used to space the fender away from the tire.

You can also use spacer blacks or rubber hose along the tire curve, but I prefer the towel method as it inhibits the fender from wobbling side-to-side when placed for aligning. The fender is then aligned in the position it will be mounted forward or back. The front of the fender will be secured with two bolts that will fasten it to the frame's fender mount tab.

When the fender is properly positioned on the wheel and towel, I indicate the drill-out points with a grease pencil (Fig. 3-27).

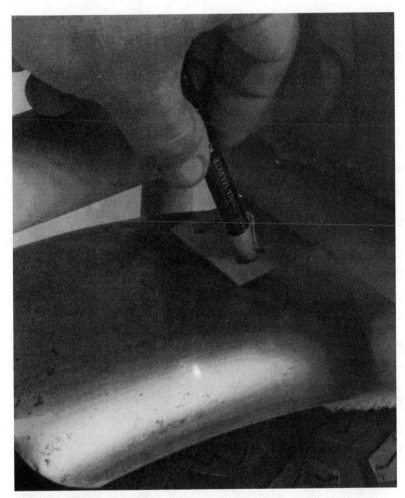

Tab mounting hole locations are determined and marked off with a grease pencil. They will then be drilled out to accommodate ¼-inch mounting bolts.

As a further alignment check, I measure from the end of the forward part of the fender (Fig. 3-28). Holes are then drilled out. Since ⅜-inch bolts are used for mounting, I used a ⅜-inch drill bit. Measurement should be as exacting as possible. As a safety measure, you might want to drill out one hole a little longer— say, ¼ inch—so that if you are a little off, the fender can be jockeyed into more positive alignment prior to tightening down the bolts.

Once the drilling is done, the fender can be mounted to the frame tab. In virtually all cases, flat fenders need to be spaced from the tab and this requires the insertion of spacers between

3-28
Careful measuring will determine proper centering and fender alignment. Centerline of fender is indicated by the black dot.

the tab and fender (Fig. 3-29). You can cut spacers from ¼-inch diameter tube stock after measuring the distance between fender and frame tab, or, as I did, use standard ¼-inch spacers. My installation required two ¼-inch spacers to gap a ½-inch span. The final step in securing the forward portion of the fender is to tighten down the bolts. I strongly recommend using lock washers to inhibit bolt-loosening due to vibrations induced by the bike.

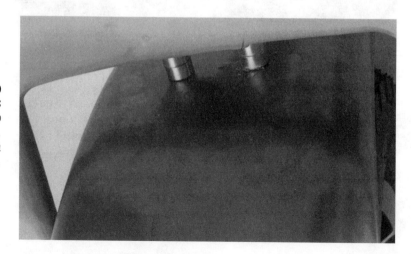

3-29
The use of spacers is almost always necessary to achieve proper fender height. Here two ¼-inch aluminum spacers accomplish the job.

The rear or central portion of the fender must also be secured. On a hardtail frame, the conventional methods are to use brackets (from fender to frame) or a sissy rail, which can also serve to secure the fender. I chose the latter method (Fig. 3-30). The most critical aspect of mounting a free fender of this type lies in positioning and securing the front part of the fender (Fig. 3-31).

Flat fenders are considered custom accessory add-ons and must be custom-mounted. The greater part of aftermarket accessory fenders are either replacement items or produced to bolt on to existing Harley frames and frame tabs.

Mounting front fenders on springer front ends can be tricky due to the up-and-down rocker motion of the springers. This has resulted in high-mounted front fenders, which give an "off-road bike" appearance in the front—definitely not conducive to good custom aesthetics (Fig. 3-32). Master innovative parts genius Wyatt Fuller has evolved a foolproof method of springer fender mounting primarily designed for Harley front springers. Kuryakin produces and markets the kit.

3-30
Sissy rail fender bracket serves to secure the rear of the accessory fender.

3-31
The fender installation complete.

3-32
The problem:
Stock fender mounting.

3-33
The solution:
Kuryakin fender
lowering kit.

A similar kit will be marketed by Paughco for all accessory springers (Fig. 3-33). With minor modifications to the Harley springer shown here, the lowering device, which works in unison with the lower rocker movement, can be mounted in a matter of an hour or two. Here's how it's done:

First, the disk caliper unit is removed from the springer and set aside (Fig. 3-34).

3-34
Remove the brake caliper.

The stock factory springer fender mount tabs must then be sawed off with a hacksaw as shown here (Fig. 3-35). Next, the two fender mounting telescopic sleeves provided in the kit are fitted over the nubs remaining when the original mount plates are cut off (Fig. 3-36).

After the sleeves are secured with an Allen wrench, the slider mechanisms of the kit are attached (Fig. 3-37). The kit's rocker slider legs are then affixed to the lower rockers and the slider unit (Fig. 3-38). The fender is now permanently secured to the

3-35
Cutting the stock factory fender mount.

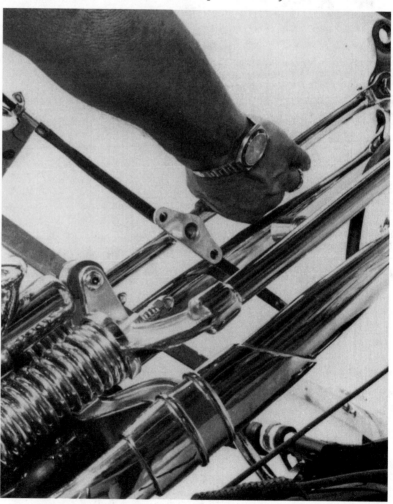

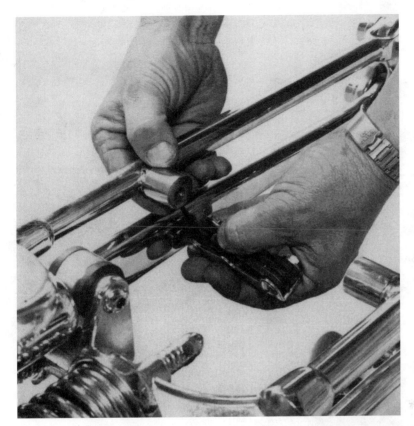

3-36
Mounting sleeves are placed on stock Harley nubs remaining after cutting fender mount tabs.

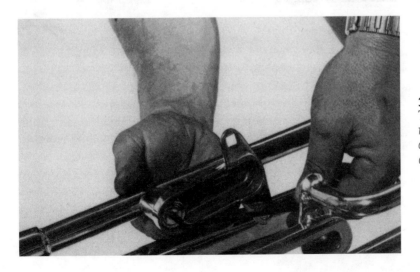

3-37
The slide mechanism is now attached. Slider rides on two Delrin bushings and a Ny-lock bolt.

Fenders & tanks 81

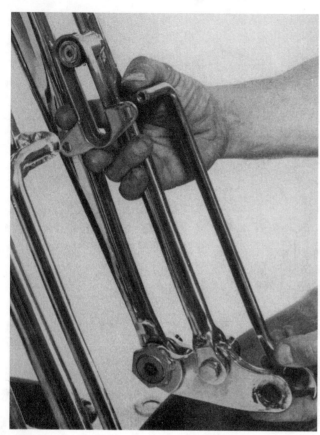

3-39
*Fender is bolted down
with bolts going through the fender holes
and into the slider plate and rocker
assembly.*

3-38
The lower rocker leg is attached to the slider plate.

sliding mounting bracket. A single bolt is utilized to secure the fender and affix the sliding leg at the same time (Fig. 3-39). The slide unit itself rides on two Delrin bushings and a Ny-loc bolt all supplied in the kit. Before replacing the wheel, the axle must be modified simply and easily by adding the special axle sleeve bushings provided, one on each side as shown in Fig. 3-40 to allow uninhibited rocker operation. Securing the axle and wheel assembly completes the installation (Fig. 3-41).

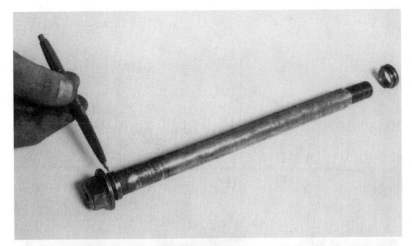

3-40
Special sleeves are telescoped over the axle to serve as rocker leg bushings. A special sleeve is provided for the right side and one for the left.

3-41
After axle and wheel are slipped back into place, the axle nut is tightened.

The fender lowering kit is the only feasible fender mounting method applicable to springer mounting that allows the fender to sit close to the wheel without interfering with up-and-down rocker action. It's a welcome aftermarket accessory that revolutionizes front fender mounting for springer units (Fig. 3-42).

3-42
Mounted lowering kit.

"American Excess." Owner: John Morton.
Paint: Dawn of Air-Craft, Fort Lauderdale, Fla.

Danny Giafaglione's 1986 Softail FXST.
Builder: Wyatt Fuller.
Paint: Dawn of Air-Craft.

"Hog High." 1984 FXST.
Owner: Dave Lumsden.
Paint: Dawn of Air-Craft.

Detail of artwork on
the tank of "Hog High."

1989 Harley Softail Springer.
Builder: Wyatt Fuller.
Graphics: Dawn of Air-Craft.
Powder coating of engine: Sumax.

Felix Lugo's "Intimidation."
Nitrous-oxide-boosted
1972 XLH Sportster.
Engine work: John Sachs.
Builder: Phantom Motorcycles,
Oakland Park, Fla.

1984 Custom Shovelhead.
Owner–builder: Joe Ferraro of
Brothers III, Pompano Beach, Fla.
Paint: Spike, Orlando, Fla.

Bob Merlino's "Florida Flyer,"
1989 Softail Springer.
Owner–builder: Brothers III.
Paint: Frank Cali.

Turbo Tom's turbocharged, fuel-injected FXST Softail. Builder: Scott Baringer and Jim Camene of Custom Accessories, Pompano Beach, Fla. Paint: Chris Cruz.

Ace Armstrong's 1991 street racer featuring Fueling-Rivera 4-valve heads. Builder: Phil Peterson's Harley-Davidson, Miami, Fla.

Detail of paintwork on rear fender of "Twisted Sisters." Paintwork and art: Carl Caiati.

Jeff Dillworth's "Twisted Sister," a 1972 FLX with 1960s chopper styling. Builder: Heaven on Wheels, Fort Lauderdale, Fla. Paint and murals: Carl Caiati.

Melinda Davis' "Pink Thing,"
1988 Harley Heritage.
Builder: Red Racing, Boca Raton, Fla.
Paint: Mike Adams.

"New Wave," 1987 FXSTC.
Owner–builder: Bob Davis and Red Racing,
Boca Raton, Fla.
Engine work: Harley-Davidson, Palm Beach.
Paint: Mike Adams.

Ron Finch's show-winning "Odin's Axel."
Closeup of infinite front fender and fork metal
work.

Finch's "Odin's Axel." Rear left side view showing
hand-machined frame axes and ornate metal
sculpturing.

(Above) View of custom-painted and
detailed sportster tank.
Paint and artwork: Carl Caiati.
(Left) Mark Shadley's show-stopping
Sportser featuring a Magnuson blower.
Engine work: Jim Thompson of
Randolph, Mass.
Paint and assembly: Dave Perowitz,
Cycle Fabrications, Brockton, Mass.

Chrome & bolt-on accessories

To UPDATE an old adage, all that glitters is not chrome. But on a Harley-Davidson, 90 percent of the time it is; customizers use chrome plating to glamorize distinctive metal parts and castings on engines as well as other functional and decorative parts (Fig. 4-1).

Sumax, Inc.

4-1
An example of engine beautification achieved by extensive chromework.

There are two approaches to chroming: Have it done professionally, or buy chrome accessory parts, the latter being the quickest and most favorable method, since many aftermarket chrome replacement parts are highly distinctive and stylized, as you will see.

Chrome accessory parts can be obtained from aftermarket Harley accessory shops and mail-order catalogs. Three good mail-order sources are Drag Specialties, Custom Chrome, Inc., and Paughco, Inc. (see Appendix for addresses). Some decorative aftermarket accessories are also available in anodized finishes such as aluminum and polished or satin metal.

Chrome plating

A great many customizers like to go this route. For one thing, you can take existing unchromed steel or aluminum parts and have them rechromed for less than the cost of a new factory-chromed accessory piece. Stock chromed parts are mass-produced items and one can have superior chrome if he will go the triple chrome plating route offered by better quality chrome platers. It is unwise to skip on costs in rechroming. Choose the best chrome plater you can find.

One way to ensure against bad plating is to use the services available at Harley or custom motorcycle shops who specialize in chrome plating services for their customers. Trying to find a good chromer on a hit-or-miss basis is not recommended. A Harley or bike shop relies on an excellent plater and most shops have established a long-term working relationship with custom platers who specialize in motorcycle parts chromework. It is unlikely that a plater affiliated with a bike shop will deal off bad chrome; they take a chance of losing the shop to another plater. Though chrome plating shops are not found all over, those that exist are very competitive with each other and the key to a flourishing relationship between plater and bike shop is quality. So if you are looking for quality chromework, go to a reputable custom or Harley shop.

The degree of flawless finishing on chrome parts is dependent on the condition of the metal piece to be chromed. It must be rust-free, not excessively pitted or gouged, and not have casting cracks; all these conditions detract from the appearance and adhesion of chrome. Since motorcycle chrome must hold up to weather conditions and road wear and tear, only triple chrome plating will do. In triple chrome plating, first a layer of copper must be applied to the metal piece. The initial copper coating serves to coat the entire piece and fill in nicks, pits and scratches. The copper works in the same fashion as a prime coat on a paint job. Before the piece is plated it is sandblasted, degreased, and, if necessary, buffed to rough out the base so that the copper will adhere (Fig. 4-2).

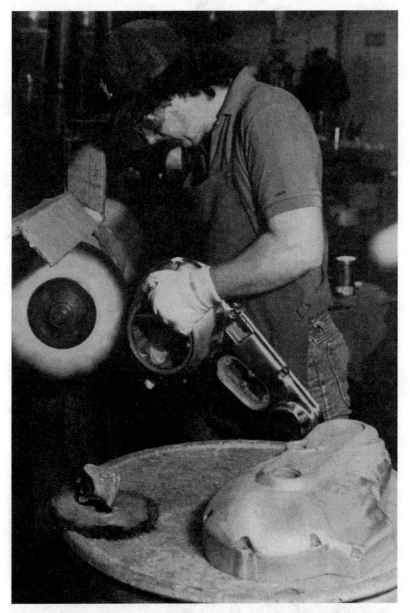

4-2
Prior to plating, parts must be bead-blasted, prepped, and buffed as shown here to be ready for electro-plating. Copper plating is the first step.

A copper base coat of at least .005 is required. After the copper coating process, the polisher will remove enough of the copper buildup to eliminate the surface imperfections. When the piece attains the lustre of a shiny new penny, it's ready for the second plating step, nickel plating (Fig. 4-3). This step is akin to color coating or base coating in painting. After heavy nickel plating, a coat of chrome plating is administered, which finishes off the piece much like a final clear coat in painting gives the surface its shine and lustre (Fig. 4-4). When the piece is finished and properly chromed, an additional buildup of .015 to .020 inch covers the chromed component. The more complex the part or surface irregularities encountered (corners, edges, recessions), the longer the plating process. Not all parts require the same plating time or buildup, but generally speaking, the entire procedure from start to finish can involve four to six hours to complete. Most of the work is in the preparatory procedure prior to each plating step.

4-3
After the part is copper plated and buffed again, it is dipped into the nickel plating vat shown here.

4-4
The final step in the process is chrome plating, wherein the piece achieves its dazzling chrome luster.

The better the surface condition of the piece to be chromed, the better and more lustrous the chroming attained. Finished chromework should be cleaned and polished regularly in order for it to maintain its lustre. Special chrome polishing agents such as Simichrome are specifically formulated for chrome surface polishing and preservation.

Chrome & bolt-on accessories 89

Mounting chromed pieces

Though chroming assists in the preservation of the chromed piece, it must be understood that the process consists of laying a coating of chrome over the metal in an electrical process that bonds to the polished top coating, which is actually laid over two other metal plated surfaces for proper adhesion. You cannot just plate over bare metal or aluminum; the process must rely on the intermediate metal coating process for the successful application and longevity of the chrome.

Since the chrome is a metallized film, it can crack if the metal piece plated flexes too much, is bent when being mounted, or too much torque is applied to mounting bolts, which will tend to allow the chrome to crack around bolt holes under excessive bolt torquing pressure. If you are mounting thin pieces or components such as chain guards, don't use excessive torque pressure and implement lockwashers to secure the chrome pieces. Thin fiber washers between bolts and chromed surfaces will also aid in inhibiting chrome cracking or breaking away around bolt mounting holes.

Chromed axles can be problematic, since they must be mounted by sliding them through wheel axle holes and bearings that are usually a tight and snug fit. When mounting rechromed or chromed axles that must be tapped into place, use an abundance of lubricant on the axle shaft and *never* tap in the chromed head bolt portion of the axle with a metal hammer. If you do, the chrome on the axle head will crack or flake away. Use a rubber mallet, and for added insurance tap the axle in with short, intermittent taps until the axle is in place. A piece of ½-inch foam covering the axle head will also help dissipate the hammer blows and further ensure against chrome chipping and cracking. Exercise care and use the properly prescribed tools when mounting chromed pieces.

Accessory chrome parts

A wide assortment of engine case and bolt-on accessory parts is marketed by major producers of engine replacement chrome parts. Custom-styled outer primary cases are available for virtually all Harley engines; some are replacement parts, some are decorative (Fig. 4-5).

4-5
A typical aftermarket accessory chrome piece is this 1970 to 1984 FX Case cover. These items are marketed by CCI and Drag Specialties.

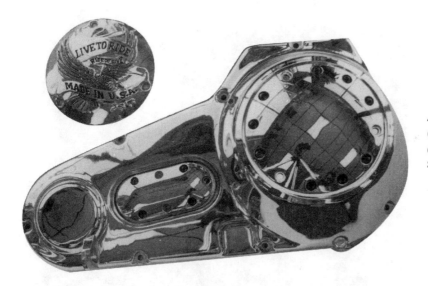

4-6
Good show chrome exhibits a mirror-like glass luster as shown here.

These parts are easily mounted by removing the old parts and bolting on the new ones with stock hardware or accessory refined bolts that come with the parts. Chrome add-on parts are numerous and plentiful, and you need only to peruse the aftermarket chrome catalogs to see what is available to suit your individual taste. Even sundry engine parts can be obtained to glamorize and individualize the engine (Figs. 4-6 through 4-8).

4-7

Some popular chrome air cleaner add-ons. (A) Drilled disc for Bendix, Keihin S & S and Tillotson carbs; (B) Round air cleaner for standard Harley carbs as listed in A; (C) Wedge air cleaner cover for all Bendix, Keihin carbs; (D) Turbo-styled cleaner cover will fit most Bendix, Tillotson, Mikuni, S.U. and Keihin carbs.

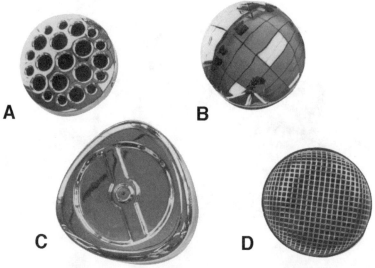

A   B

C   D

4-8
Drag Specialties DS-289050 Dragon II air cleaner.

You can do much to enhance your engine's aesthetics by replacing simple parts such as pushrod covers (Fig. 4-9) or adding little simple chrome touches dispersed around the engine (Fig. 4-10). The rear axle mounting nuts on the Softail Harley were always prominent and ugly. To beautify the Softail suspension's axle and segments, Harley provides their chromed Softail axle covers for 1982–92 Harley Softail models (Fig. 4-11).

4-9
Pushrod cover design created by Wyatt Fuller is marketed by Sumax Inc.

4-10
Another Wyatt Fuller innovation: Fire dome chromed spark plug caps for all Harleys. They're marketed by Kuryakin.

4-11
Swingarm axle covers for Harley Softail frames for all 86 to 92 Softail models.

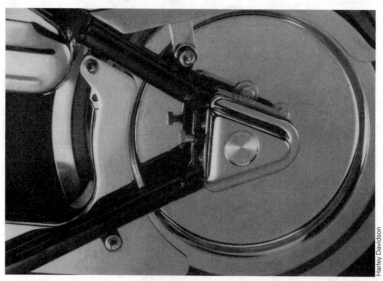

Harley Davidson

Another version is offered by Kuryakin, highly stylized chromed axle covers with show-quality design that bolt on with no modifications necessary in a matter of minutes (Figs. 4-12, 4-13).

4-12
Yet another Wyatt Fuller custom creation is the Softail Phantom Cover available from Kuryakin. It's a one-two-three bolt-on item which covers axle and retaining nut.

4-13
Harley-Davidson makes available these stylish belt drive rotor covers for belt-drive models.

A number of aftermarket Harley-Davidson oil tanks are offered to upgrade the looks of the street or show Harley. They are available in round, horseshoe, and various geometric shapes in triple chrome plated coatings. They are, for the most part, custom-fabricated with perfectly contoured and fine-finished facets. All of these aftermarket offerings are bolt-on replacement parts for stock issues and are made for virtually all Harley-Davidson motorcycle models (Fig. 4-14, 4-15).

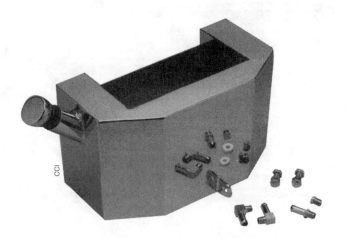

4-14
From Custom Chrome (CCI), custom wedge oil tank for custom frame adaption.

Chrome & bolt-on accessories 95

4-15
Another custom oil tank, for FX and FL model Harleys accepts standard FXE Battery.

Drag Specialties

A wide array of side pipes is marketed, many of them custom-designed for optimum looks and performance. The proper selection of side pipes to fit in with the overall look of your Harley will do much to enhance its appearance. A few popular versions are illustrated here (Figs. 4-16, 4-17). The hot setups today are the fishtail pipes. A throwback to the 1950s and '60s, fishtail pipes are making a big comeback and can be seen on many current street machines. A wide assortment of pipes is marketed by CCI, Drag Specialties, Paughco, Inc., and Sumax Inc. (Fig. 4-18).

4-16
CCI tapered-style dyno-powered shotgun pipes for rigid frames. Fits all 1966 to 1969 early Shovels in rigid frames.

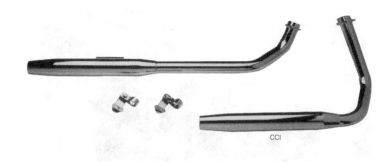

CCI

4-17
Drag Specialties' turnout mufflers for FLT, FLHT, 1980 to 1989.

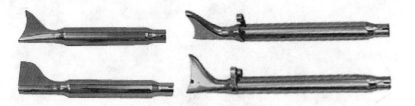

4-18
*Classic fishtail pipes are
manufactured by Paughco Inc.*

Handlebars are frequently changed by riders who wish to
upgrade riding comfort or handlebar reach. Many styles and
types are offered to suit each individual's taste (Figs. 4-19
through 4-21).

Custom risers are also available for front ends; these aid in
raising handlebars to selective heights and positions. The risers
will bolt onto glide and springer front ends (Figs. 4-22, 4-23).

The catalogs and accessories dealers abound in accessory
footpegs. They are marketed in a variety of styles and finishes,
some streamlined and others massive for positive foot resting
and placement. Stock footpegs are often replaced by custom
builders, as stock issues are seldom as attractive as aftermarket
types (Figs. 4-24 through 4-26).

Chrome chain guards are very popular and many are offered in
stylized versions. Slimmed down, racy versions are offered as
well as louvered and perforated examples; the custom
accessory catalogs abound in chain guard models (Fig. 4-27).

Last but not least, the easiest custom touch that can be added
is the custom gas cap. Almost all bikes will sport them soon
after hitting the pavement, as there is nothing uglier or more
common-looking than a stock gas cap. Harley, as well as the
leading aftermarket accessory manufacturers, offers myriad
assorted gas caps to embellsh the fat-bob, sportster, or
accessory custom tanks. They come with Harley emblems
(which are very popular), with fluted and grooved edges, with
bullet and faceted protrusions, or in a few flat chromed
versions (Fig. 4-28).

4-19
Sixties-style high bars—
"apehanger"-style
pullbacks—can be obtained
from such sources as CCI and
Drag Specialties.

4-20
Very popular today are the
Buckhorn bars issued by
Drag Specialties.

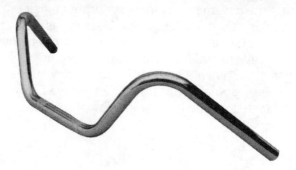

4-21
The drag-style bars and chromed domed risers are specialty bars issued by CCI.

4-22
These novel and unique risers are straight from the Harley-Davidson chrome accessory catalog.

4-23
These unique novelty design risers are from CCI. Other distinctively designed risers can be obtained from Drag Specialties.

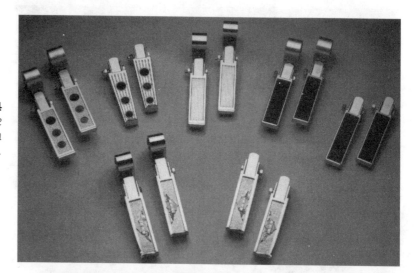

4-24
Accessory footpegs are available from such sources as CCI.

4-25
The top two units are from Drag Specialties. Shown are ISO kick (top) and foot pegs. The two bottom units are from CCI, including foot peg and kick starter peg (bottom).

4-26
This foot peg heel rest design is by Wyatt Fuller; it helps to alleviate foot fatigue on long-distance rides. Manufacturer is Kuryakin.

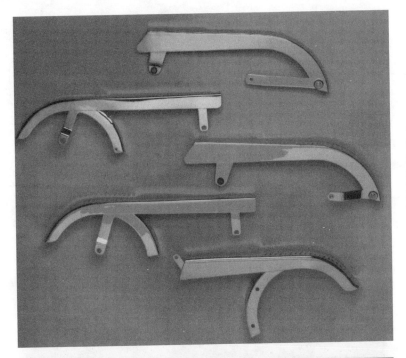

4-27
Custom Chrome (CCI) offers a host of chain guards, smooth or louvered for FL, FX, XL and FXR model Harleys 1973 to present.

4-28
Gas caps abound from CCI to add a custom touch to stock gas tanks.

As an alternative to chrome parts, there are other machined or coated parts that are favorably accented and initiated into the decor of custom motorcycles. Some folks like billet aluminum parts for their subtle satin luster and custom machined excellence. CCI, Drag Specialties, and Sumax, Inc. offer a host of these highly decorative goodies (Fig. 4-29). If color is your thing, you might opt for anodized or powder-coated aluminum accessories and sundries. Some highly refined pieces are exhibited here (Figs. 4-30, 4-31).

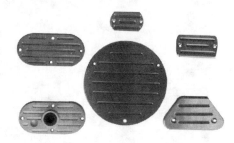

4-29
Machined billet aluminum is a current rage for primary inspection and derby covers. These satin-finished luxury items are supplied by CCI.

4-30
Engraved and powder-coated pushrod covers are a specialty of Sumax Inc.

4-31
Sumax also features primary and inspection covers powder-coated and engraved.

These components can be added to contemporary and older Harleys with the aid of simple hand tools. Accessories are predesigned and fitted for various Harley-Davidson motorcycles and can be obtained from such sources as Custom Chrome, Inc., Drag Specialties, Paughco, Inc., Arlen Ness Enterprises, Gary Lang, Inc., and Jammer Cycle Products. All of these sources offer fully illustrated catalogs featuring their offerings and showing how the parts mount on the various Harley models. Excellent mounting instructions are also provided to aid the customizer in mounting each component. See the Appendix for supplier addresses.

Body exchange & bolt-on items

Lights

All bikes require regulation headlights, taillights, and running lights, which are mandatory for legal road operation of the vehicle. To enhance or customize a bike, many owners will opt to add to or change the lighting configurations.

In many cases, installation involves a simple swap and hookup to the existing electrical wiring or wiring harnesses of the motorcycle's electrical system (Fig. 4-32). For the most part, they can be screwed on or bolt-fastened onto fenders, rails, bars, and so forth with the aid of a screwdriver or small wrench. Occasionally, you will need to drill out mounting holes to hold the lights or light brackets.

4-32
Dozens of accessory lights are marketed by the major accessory sources.

In addition to accessory units, there are also stock units that you might want to install or swap. With all the stock and accessory lights available, the possibilities are virtually inexhaustible.

Some customizers choose basic minimal lighting setups to fit in with the aesthetics of the bike. Others take a more radical route, if the bike will accommodate this approach without distorting its looks. Owners of street cruisers termed "garbage wagons" will sometimes install batteries or groups of lights, since the bulk of the overall bike will accommodate them (Figs. 4-33, 4-34). Multiple lighting setups as shown here usually apply to big cruisers and add to the aesthetic impact.

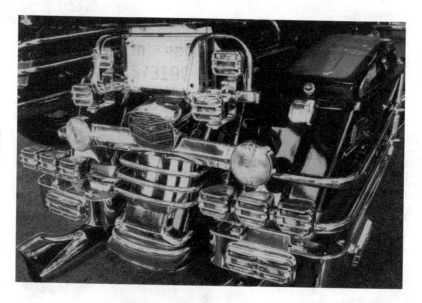

4-33
An example of a well-lighted rear end on a street dresser.

Sissy rails

Sissy rails enjoyed their greatest popularity in the 1960s era of custom biking, when choppers were the rage. At that time they were made by custom fabricators, but soon were copied by custom accessory manufacturers that realized the potential market.

The sissy rail's primary function was a passenger backrest, but they also contributed to the overall aesthetics of the bike. Some were basic, moderately styled units; others were bizarre and

4-34
*Another rear end rendering
uses a cluster of bullet lights.*

outrageous. The ultra-high sissy rail-seat combination made
for a great, laid-back ride for passengers, but could cause some
unstable handling in high crosswinds. Occasionally, you will
see a few of these types around, but they are not as fashionable
or desired today (Figs. 4-35, 4-36).

Today, sissy rails are more moderate in styling and height, and
various aftermarket bolt-on rails are marketed by the leading

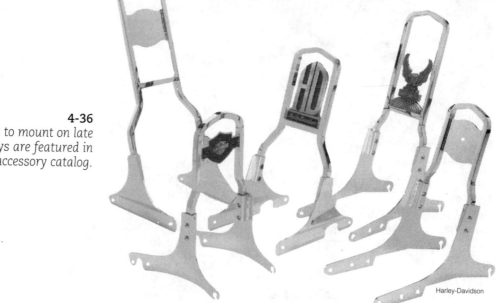

4-35
This FXD Dyna chrome sport luggage rack is available from Harley-Davidson; fits all 91 and 92 FXD Dyna Glide models with H-D sissy bar upright side plates.

Harley-Davidson

4-36
Sissy rails to mount on late model Harleys are featured in the Harley accessory catalog.

Harley-Davidson

106 Customizing Your Harley

accessory manufacturers. The only elaborate, ornate, or oversized versions are relegated to custom show machinery, and they are custom-made. The accessory mass-marketed contemporary sissy rail is designed along modular concepts and can be added on or removed and changed at will with little fuss or muss. Rail size configurations are between eight and 14 inches above the seat and will accept accessory or OEM (original equipment manufacturer) decorative sissy bar inserts.

Harley-Davidson offers an array of emblems and eagles that will fit into their units or can be easily adapted into aftermarket accessory rails (see Chapter 9 on ornamentation). Custom Chrome, Inc., offers a variety of styles built around custom steel side-mounting plates that fit on current Harley fender supports. On the inside of the side plates are mounting channels for the grab rail, and uprights contain mounting screws that access from the rear of the bike. This feature simplifies the changing of one grab rail style to another, high or low, and the various modular components will interchange from one Harley to another. Other manufacturers offer similar universal mounting systems.

A few sissy rails must be custom mounted by drilling and bolting onto frames, but virtually all the commercial sissy bars produced today will bolt into place with adapters for various swing and rigid frames made available by several manufacturers.

For a clean mounted look and easy removal, Kuryakin, a latecomer to the accessory aftermarket, with the aid of master designer Wyatt Fuller developed a new, easy rail mount relying on the patented Kuryakin-style "quickie plates." These allow a sissy rail to be installed or removed in seconds with simple hand tools (Fig. 4-37).

The mounting plates will accept many factory or aftermarket sissy bars and are installed by removing the four strut bolts on the Harley, replacing them with four specially designed bolts provided in the Hog Style kit (Fig. 4-38). The sissy rail is then affixed to the mounting plates. To secure the sissy rail and mounting plates to the bike, the front plate sections are slid

4-37
Quick-release design sissy rail kit by Wyatt Fuller allows quick removal in a simple clip-on system.

4-38
Rail can be completely removed without major alteration to the stock Harley struts.

over the front bolts (Fig. 4-39), and the spring-loaded locknuts situated at the rear of the plates are twisted, releasing the spring pressure and securing the sissy rail mounting plate unit. Removal is achieved by reversing the procedure.

4-39
Spring-release knob allows quick removal, allowing the unit to be disengaged.

Kuryakin quickie plates are available for all Harley-Davidson Softail models, early FX and FL models, and late FXRs and Sportsters. All the kits are available with or without turn signal cutouts.

Not all current accessory sissy rail offerings are of the quick-mount type, even though they are bolt-ons. In some instances, such as with custom hardtail frames, it will be necessary to place-fit the rail unit, then drill out the rail mount tab and the end tail frame plate to secure the sissy rail unit.

The longer-than-average sissy rails designed for hardtail frames are fully chromed and finished, with the end areas welded to square stock long enough for universal mounting to all Harley or aftermarket rigid frames. These rarely if ever have to be shortened. They are positioned in place and clamped on the side opposite to the one to be drilled, then a hole is drilled

4-40
Mounting a high sissy rail to a rigid frame requires drilling into the tailpiece as shown. The rail is further secured by a bolt fastening the fender to the fender strut, which is part of the rail unit.

through the sissy bar mounting section and the frame tail plate. The fender is rested on the rail crossmember that goes under the fender (Fig. 4-40). The crossmember of the rail serves a dual purpose: It mounts and secures the fender, and allows the fender to secure the sissy rail at the same time. Sissy rails can be securely mounted with ¼×1-inch bolts (Fig. 4-41).

CCI

4-41
Modular Custom Chrome sissy bars can be swapped onto their universal bases without sideplate removal. Bases accept various CCI rail designs.

Seats

Seats are a matter of personal preference and, it seems, one of the earliest and most frequent accessory items considered. There are a number of seats marketed that offer improved styling and comfort.

Seat styling had radically changed in the past 20 years, though some styles have become obsolete. The new lowrider look is in, and most of the offerings today reflect this styling. Low-profile frame and fender contouring make the plush seat and pillion combination a favored accessory seating item.

Occasionally, a replacement seat will be custom-upholstered to color-match or enhance the overall theme of the bike, and this requires the somewhat costly services of a custom upholsterer. Unfortunately, custom seats come only in black and basically tufted or pleated to keep costs down (Figs. 4-42 through 4-44).

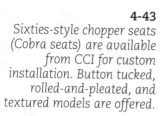
4-42
Two-up Corbin Gunfighter seat for FXR models.

4-43
Sixties-style chopper seats (Cobra seats) are available from CCI for custom installation. Button tucked, rolled-and-pleated, and textured models are offered.

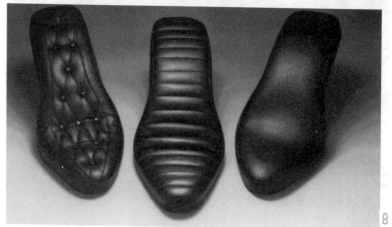

4-44
The popular DS-905990 pillow one-piece in regular stitched or pillow versions by Drag Specialties fits all '84 to '89 FXST models.

Nearly all aftermarket seats fabricated for Harleys feature bolt-on installation; the hardware included will allow the seat to be quickly attached to existing Harley seat fixtures. A number of them will be interchangeable, and catalogs offered by the major aftermarket accessory manufacturers providing seats indicate the mounting configurations for their seats.

Occasionally, you might want to mount a seat not designed for your particular Harley model. This will mean modifying the seat or the frame mount fixtures—preferably the seat units, which can be adapted with a little modification ingenuity. The seat chosen in this example for mounting onto a Harley Sportster hardtail frame was the Drag Specialties one-piece Solo and pillion seat. This seat is designed to mount on 1985 and later FXST Harley-Davidsons.

To secure the front of the seat by the tab or tongue under the Drag Specialties seat, I first had to fabricate a bracket (Fig. 4-45). The bracket was cut ¾-inch wide from 1¾-inch channel

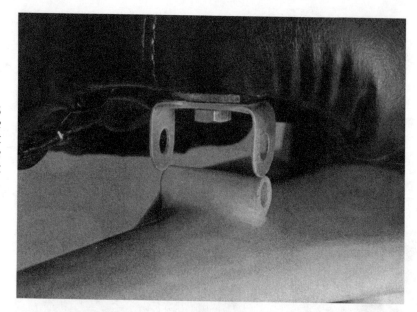

4-45
In the custom rigid frame installation, a special bracket is first made to secure the front of the seat to the seat mount tube.

stock. Steel stock is best, with a thickness of ⅟₁₆-inch. You can round the corners, as I did, or leave them square. Drill holes in the sidewalls and in the center of the bracket for mounting to the mounting tongue under the accessory seat. The fashioned bracket is then affixed to the tongue by drilling a ⅜-inch hole in the tongue and attaching the bracket by means of a ⅜-x½-inch nut and bolt (Fig. 4-46).

The plate under the seat, at the rear of the pillion section, contains a threaded hole and will accommodate a ⅜-inch bolt for mounting the back portion of the seat to a rear fender (Fig. 4-47). The seat rear is secured to the fender via one of these holes by drilling a mounting hole in the fender. You can indicate the location of the hole on the side of the seat with chalk by putting the seat in place, marking the side of the fender, then drawing a line across the fender width to determine the mounting hole location. The hole can be drilled a bit oversized for flexibility in seat placement if your hole is a little off. You can see in Fig. 4-48 what the modified seat looks like mounted to the frame. In many instances, alterations in seat mounting procedures are required to adapt a particular seat to a certain frame.

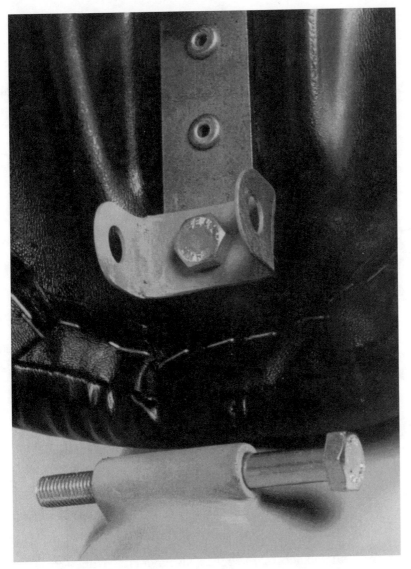

4-46
The bracket, secured by a bolt to the tongue, is held in place by the long bolt going through the seat mount tube.

Wheels

The original Harley wheel is the spoked type, which has remained the traditional motorcycle wheel. Spoked wheels do need a checkup and maintenance every once in a while, as the spokes can loosen with excessive use. This is one reason why the contemporary cast mags have gained in popularity. They are usually one-piece, perfectly cast wheels that remain true while needing no adjustments such as spoke tightening and

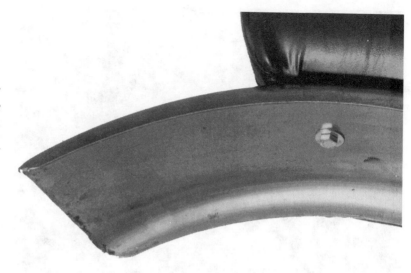

4-47
The rear pillion section of the seat secures to the fender via a second bolt going into a pre-installed threaded retainer built into the seat base plate.

4-48
The completed seat installation.

truing. Twisted accessory spokes, also available from accessory chrome sources, can contribute to the looks and distinctiveness of spoked wheels. Truing and respoking of wheels should be undertaken by qualified experts or shops that have the necessary equipment.

The revolutionary Rev-Tech chromed wheels illustrated here are forged in aluminum, combining superior strength and lower weight. They are even lighter than laced wheels. The lighter weight offers minimal rotating mass, which provides a smoother ride and better acceleration and handling.

After the rim halves are cold forged, they are fastened to the hub with Grade 8 hardware, then placed in accurate jigs while they are welded together in the rim well area. The wheels are then machined on a CNC (computer numerically controlled) lathe to ensure runout accuracy within 0.010 inch. The cutouts are also machined on the CNC mill to guarantee accuracy and consistency.

Custom Chrome

4-49
Rev-Tech wheels of forged polished aluminum for Harley models 1978 to present. Left to right: Rev-Lite, Rev-Pro, Rev-Star, Rev-Star Directional.

CCI

4-50
Great wheel touches. CCI chrome front wheel hubcaps for FL's and Softails. Will fit 1984 and up FXST, FLST, FXWG, and also 1981 thru 84 FL models with cast wheels.

Chrome & bolt-on accessories 117

These wheels can run either tubed or tubeless tires, another positive factor. Each wheel features Timken bearings with proper preload set at the factory, and comes complete with all necessary spacers. The fine-polished wheels do not require constant repolishing and maintenance and will not fade, oxidize, or corrode as traditional wheels can (Figs. 4-49 through 4-51).

4-51
Harley mag wheels are great in the looks department on either customs or stockers.

Pinstriping & lettering

ONE CUSTOM TOUCH that will clearly set your Harley-Davidson apart from all others is the use of graphic design enhancements such as pinstriping and lettering. *True* pinstriping is applied with a brush. Tape striping, often incorrectly referred to as pinstriping, involves applying an auto stripe tape. The purist relies strictly on hand striping, even though the difference is subtle to most. Lettering, for the most part, is also applied by brush, but in cases where it is to be sealed under clear paint, sprayed topcoats and other special effects can be executed with an airbrush. The lettering segment within this chapter covers the use of both.

Pinstriping

The art of decorative pinstriping dates back to horse-and-buggy days, when coaches were accented with line striping. Today, pinstriping is a popular design element for motorcycles, as well as automobiles and trucks, since the areas on bikes (tanks, fenders, and frames) are relatively small and confined, making them easy to fill with decorative line and scrollwork.

Though hand pinstriping is not an easy craft to master, expertise can be acquired with periodic practice. Application techniques can be mastered within six months if you are willing to devote the time, practice, and patience.

Pinstriping tools

To hand-pinstripe your Harley, you will need dagger brushes to apply the paint, and paint made specifically for striping (Fig. 5-1).

Specially designed for pinstriping, dagger brushes are short brushes with bristles as long as or longer than the handles. When wet or paint-laden, the bristles are similar in profile to a dagger, hence the name "dagger brush." They come in various

The basic necessities for pinstriping a bike are paint and brushes. Two popular striping paints are Sign Painters' One-Shot and House of Kolor urethane enamel. Brushes are the dagger type specifically designed for striping, as they hold large amounts of paint for long-line striping.

sizes from 00 to 5, the 00 size being the most commonly used for fine linework such as motorcycle striping and scrollwork. Dagger brushes can be obtained from art supply or automotive paint supply stores.

Simmons, Grumbacher, and Mack are brand names commonly available. Mack dagger brushes are of the highest quality, as are the German Langnickels. They are composed of good quality squirrel hair, are structurally sound and long-lasting, and feature round handles. Round-handled pinstriping brushes are preferred because they can be spun or rotated between the fingers during striping, a technique that is essential for circular and scrollwork striping. With the dagger brush, the wider part of the bristle stores the paint in larger quantity than a conventional paintbrush. The point of the bristle is the working segment of the brush; it determines the line width and lays down the stripe.

The two most popular striping paints are one-shot alkyd enamel and urethane enamel. Alkyd enamel requires turpentine and mineral spirits for thinning; urethane enamel must be thinned with urethane reducer.

For pinstriping over finished paintwork (factory or custom), one-shot enamel is ideal. It can be applied over lacquer, urethane-finished and, when dry, becomes permanent with a not-too-noticeable relief image.

Urethane enamel is the newest pinstripe paint medium and is ideal for applying on repainted finishes prior to final clear-coating. Clear-coating over urethane pinstriping gives the highest degree of permanence, since it embeds the striped graphics within the clear-coat. The finest urethane enamel specifically designed for this type of striping is Jon Kosmoski's Kosmic color enamel, made by Kosmoski's House of Kolor, Minneapolis, Minnesota (see Appendix for address).

Striping application

The first and easiest step to master in pinstriping is paint mixing. Striping paint must be properly thinned so that the brush will render fine, clean lines. If the paint is overladen with thinner, the result will be weak, less-opaque lines, or the paint can run or sag to the line edges. One test to see if the paint is too thin is to hold the brush point-down. If paint collects or forms a droplet on the tip, it is too thin. If the paint is too viscous or straight from the can, it can "dry-brush"; that is, it might not deposit an even, full, streakless line. These problems can be reconciled by adding either more thinner or more paint, whichever is required.

To properly mix the paint solution, it must be palletized (Fig. 5-2). This is accomplished by dipping the brush into the thinning solution and saturating the bristles. Then the bristles are dipped completely in paint. The brush is then wiped back and forth over a piece of paper or cardboard in a lapping motion, allowing the paint and thinner solution to intermingle until it reaches a proper consistency. You can test this as you go along. The longer you palletize, the more the paint thickens, so you must practice until you arrive at a happy medium. Palletizing is easy to master and once you have it down pat, it becomes automatic.

The striping stance

The second step that must be mastered is proper hand position for steady, controlled line execution and width. In the position, the last two fingers of the hand act as "outriggers" and can raise and lower the brush tip, which governs the width of the stripe. The more point area contacting the surface, the thicker the line, and vice versa. The chosen height must remain constant in order to execute an even-width line.

5-2
The paint thinner solution must be mixed by palletizing, or dipping the brush in thinner and then painting and stroking the brush as shown to allow the two to mix to a proper striping consistency.

The brush itself is held with the first three fingers of the hand in the same manner as a pencil. The pinkie finger may also be extended outward to contact a body line or component guideline to guide the pinstripe parallel to that bodyline, be it a fender edge, tank edge, or whatever.

To achieve a straight line, the outriggers and heel of the hand are slid along the surface being striped as the brush is held steady at a uniform height (Fig. 5-3). Straight-line striping can be easily mastered with practice.

5-3
For straight-line striping, the bottom of the palm is held against the surface, the two last fingers of the hand serving as outriggers to regulate the height of the brush to the surface to control line width.

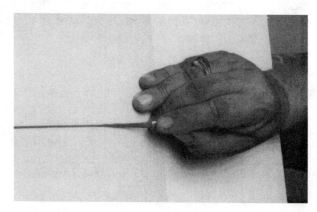

The ability to draw curved lines follows naturally, once you have gotten straight-line basics down pat. Curved lines are a bit more complex, however; a controlled brush technique is necessary to keep the pinstripes even in width as curves are negotiated. As the curve is executed, the brush must be twirled or spun a fraction. This is to keep the brush-tip hairs from fanning out as you follow the curve (Figs. 5-4, 5-5).

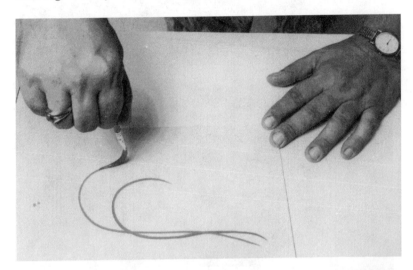

5-4
When painting along a curve, the handle must be twisted as the radius is negotiated. This keeps the brush tip hairs together so the curved line will be even.

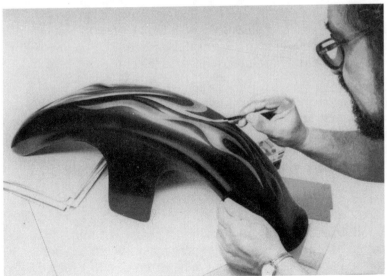

5-5
Fingertips are used to hold the brush tip off the fender to get a line of equal width. Here, flames get the edge-stripe treatment.

In the example, you can see how I edge-stripe a graphic pattern on a fender. My fourth finger rests against the surface, which helps me maintain brush-tip line width governed by the height of the brush in relation to the surface. In Fig. 5-6 you can study this operation close-up.

5-6
Close-up view of the edge striping treatment. A slow, steady stroke following the contours will guarantee a satisfactory job.

Pinstriping is not an easy process to master, but as I have mentioned before, learning it is quite feasible if you are willing to spend the time required to master the craft.

Lettering

Lettering is another decorative graphic art form often applied to motorcycles. This can take the form of a name, a slogan, or a product designation. In Fig. 5-7, "Harley-Davidson" was applied to the side panels of a Sportster tank in modern shaded type. Though this can be done by brush, I chose the airbrush technique, which is not only more striking but also part of the design motif integrated into the paint job.

For airbrush lettering, masking must be applied first. My preferred masking medium is spray mask, which can be sprayed onto the surface area to be lettered. When fully dried,

the spray mask provides a rubbery film that can be cut with an X-acto knife. The spray-mask application procedure is detailed in Chapter 6.

Lettering outlines can be laid out with a grease pencil or marker. I prefer to precut a stencil for the lettering style and size required on a piece of file-folder stock. I then transfer the stencil outline onto the spray mask with an airbrush; it's quick and easy. An alternative would be to trace out the stencil with a fine-line marker (Fig. 5-7).

Cutting out the letters on the spray-masked film is the next step. The best cutting tool to use here is an X-acto knife with a pointed #11 blade. The point negotiates curves quickly and precisely. When the letters are edge-cut, the masking can be peeled off, baring the lettering area (Fig. 5-8). An overall base color coat is then airbrushed over the lettering (Fig. 5-9). The lower part of the lettering is masked for shading by using masking tape cut and trimmed to a serrated edge. The letters are then shaded—darker at the top, fading at the bottom (Fig. 5-10).

5-8
Lettering is cut out of the spray mask. Don't use too much pressure or you will cut into the paint underneath. Apply only enough pressure to cut through the masking film.

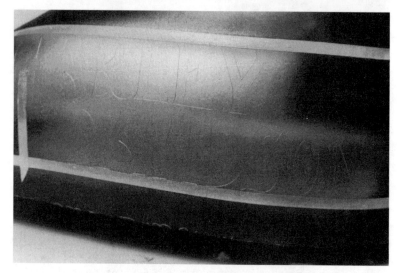

5-9
After all the letters are cut out, an overall, even airbrush coat of color is sprayed on. Three or four coats should be enough to cover, especially with metallics.

After the airbrush coloring and shading is completed, the outline spray mask is peeled off, revealing the shaded lettering motif. To finalize the artwork, the lower halves of the letters are outlined using a fine brush liner (Figs. 5-11, 5-12).

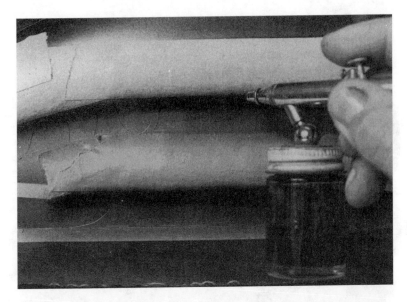

5-10
*The lettering is now shaded.
A piece of masking tape with
a serrated edge is placed
about midway to the top
area, which is masked off
with one-inch tape, as shown.*

5-11
*Lower segments of the letters
are edged to highlight them.
A fine-line artist's brush
laden with House of Kolor
striping urethane was used
for the finishing touches.*

Executed in this fashion, good, clean lettering can be applied
even by the neophyte, adding a decorative and individualistic
touch to any Harley's tanks and fenders (Fig. 5-13).

5-12
Here is a finished example of lettering work, as described in this chapter. Custom lettering can do wonders in enhancing or personalizing a paint job.

5-13
Here's another example of the airbrush-edge lettering technique on a Sportster tank.

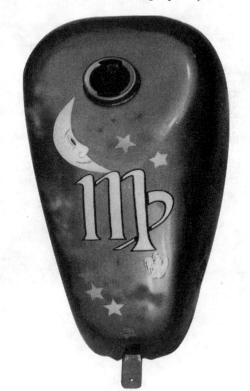

Scrollwork is a uniquely decorative technique that has been around for several years. It's currently becoming extremely popular in contemporary biking circles by such customizers as Dave Perowitz, who excels in scroll designwork. His work can be seen in Chapter 8.

Scrollwork can be applied in paint, gold leaf, or a combination of the two, depending on the customer's desires and the ingenuity of the artist. Here, I will give some basic examples of scrollwork, and show how scroll design motifs can be integrated into a paint job.

I first cut a stencil, which provides me with an exacting and finished design that can be transferred to a tank, fender, or whatever (Fig. 5-14). The stencil is essential, particularly if you wish to have identical designs on both sides of a tank, or symmetrically applied designs on a tank top, as shown. The stencil will guarantee identical design and size for each scroll section. I use spray mask exclusively for my scrollwork masking, and usually apply two coats on the tank overall.

5-14
A stencil is first cut, which will be transferred onto a spray-masked undersurface. Bristol board and simple file-folder stock make good stencil materials.

5-15
The stencil design is transferred. A grease pencil works well. Use white or yellow over a dark tank, black for dark, base-coated tanks (or painted components).

5-16
The scrollwork areas are cut out. A frisket knife will do the job, or you can use an X-acto knife with a #11 blade, as shown here.

5-17
Spray mask is peeled back to expose the areas of design to be painted. Spray mask allows fine, clean edging, a factor that makes it an ideal masking medium.

After the spray mask has fully dried to its workable rubber consistency, I trace the design onto the spraymask film (Fig. 5-15). The scroll design is then cut out using an X-acto knife. Use just enough pressure to cut through the spray mask; try not to cut through the base coat of paint underneath (Fig. 5-16). The areas to be painted are then peeled back to prepare for painting or the application of gold leaf (Fig. 5-17).

Painting scrolls

If you are going to use paint for your scrollwork (which is somewhat simpler to apply than gold leaf), I suggest applying it with an airbrush. Good gold or silver metallic base coats are marketed by the Metalflake Corporation. You can also use automotive metallics, which come in gold, silver, or any color you wish. Using the airbrush allows you to build up thin scroll design coats, thus requiring minimal clear coats to surface-finish the job (Fig. 5-18).

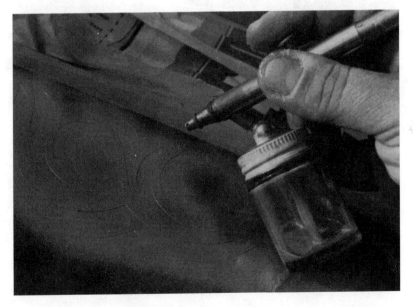

5-18
Paint scrollwork is best applied with an airbrush, which provides an even buildup of tone. Designwork and tank are then clear coated overall.

Gold leaf

Leaf scrollwork is a bit more difficult to apply, and requires care and a number of carefully executed steps in order to obtain a good gold-leaf applique finish.

Gold leaf can be purchased in art supply stores nationwide. Variegated gold leaf is most preferred, since it is heavier than straight gold leaf, hence stronger and easier to laminate on. It is also multi-hued, which makes it excitingly attractive (Fig. 5-19). Variegated composition leaf is manufactured by Houston Art and Frame Inc., in red, green, black, and blue.

5-19
Variegated gold leaf can be obtained at art supply stores. Variegated leaf has a multihued design. Adhesive is also available in spray cans for securing the leaf.

Just as with painting scrolls, for gold-leaf application you first spray mask up to the point where the design is cut, and then peel away the mask. Now a tacky substance called gold leaf *size* is applied (Fig. 5-20). This goes on in liquid form and must dry to a proper tackiness in order to secure the gold-leaf sheets that will be laid over the size. To check for the proper degree of tackiness, touch your knuckle to the sized surface (Fig. 5-21). When you pull back, you should hear a snap. This will indicate that the size is at its tack stage. If the size is too wet or not sticky, it will not dry underneath, allowing poor leaf adhesion. If it's too dry, again the leaf will not adhere properly. If you're a novice, experiment with size on a junk part before attempting a refined leaf job.

When the sizing is ready, apply the gold leaf evenly, one sheet at a time, from the bulk pack of leaf, as shown. Between each sheet is a tissue to make application easier and protect the next

sheet from damage. Gold leaf is one of the most fragile
applique media, and must be laid on with extreme care so that
it doesn't part or disintegrate as it is applied.

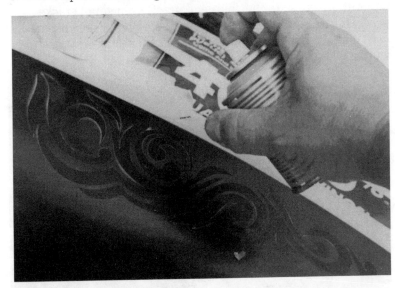

5-20
*Gold-leaf size is applied,
sprayed on in an even,
medium coat. As it dries, it
becomes tacky.*

5-21
*The knuckle test is applied to
test the tackiness of the
sizing. A proper level is
reached when you hear a
snap as you pull back from
the surface.*

Begin by laying one sheet, then slightly overlap the next until you have fully covered the sized area. Don't worry if you miss a spot; you can always place more leaf over any exposed areas without breaking up the gold-leaf effect. Even small cracks can be filled in with tiny pieces of leaf. Press down evenly on the leaf, making sure all wrinkles are smoothed. The leaf book pad works well for applying pressure evenly (Fig. 5-22).

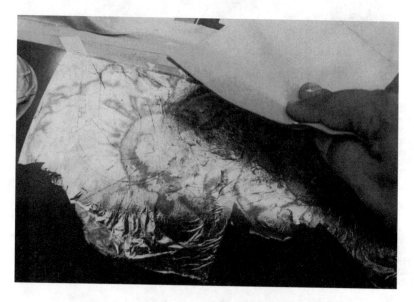

5-22
Leaf is applied from the gold-leaf book, as shown. After application, the leaf should be patted down and smoothed out.

In case you find the sizing method a bit tedious, I have discovered a better method, which I use exclusively when applying gold leaf. Instead of gold-leaf size, I use urethane or acrylic enamel clear sprayed on with a touch-up gun. One coat is sufficient. As the enamel dries, it too reaches a state of tackiness. When tacky, the leaf is applied in exactly the same manner as with sizing. This method is more foolproof than the first method. Even if you apply the leaf too early, the enamel is guaranteed to dry since the drying process is chemically activated. Of course, you must also use the required enamel catalyst. Once the enamel is cured, leaf adhesion is permanent.

After about five hours drying time regardless of the method used, the outlying spray mask can be removed, leaving the gold-leaf scroll image (Fig. 5-23).

5-23
The spray mask is removed to reveal the excellently defined scroll image. Excess gold-leaf particles can be removed with a tack rag.

In this example, a scrollwork design was created using variegated gold leaf. Variegated leaf effects are striking and are enjoying growing popularity among motorcycle customizers. With care and practice, scrollwork can be achieved by virtually anyone with artistic inclination. It is customary to apply four to five coats of lacquer or acrylic enamel clear over gold leaf for protection and permanence (Fig. 5-24).

5-24
A finished gold-leaf scroll design. Clear coating provides protection and permanence to the artwork.

Custom painting

THE CROWNING GLORY and major eye-catching feature of any custom motorcycle is the paint job. Color and design will stand out on the road, in a custom show, or even when the bike is parked in sight of onlookers. A well-executed paint job, be it conservative or flashy, will both draw attention and allow the owner to express his or her individuality.

Today, motorcycles exhibit all kinds of paint jobs—from mild to wild, subtle to bizarre, simple to complex. Graphics, murals, and other aesthetic motifs, singular or combined, are important parts of the finish of the street or show custom Harley-Davidson.

Tools

In this chapter we will cover tools, finishing systems, types of paints, and design techniques necessary to execute custom-quality paint jobs. Some of the approaches will be simple enough for a child to execute; others will be more complex. All are in the realm of the layman's expertise, however, and virtually anyone, with care and practice, can learn to paint.

Spray can

The lowly spray can is considered the poor man's painting tool, but it can be used for quality work due to the fact that motorcycle parts are small (relative to car parts) and can be covered quickly and easily with spray-can aerosols. Acrylic lacquer aerosols are the best to use for bikes and related parts, and a wide assortment of colors can be obtained from automotive paint suppliers (Fig. 6-1).

6-1
Spray cans can be used for small component painting and design work. At the left is the Pre-Val spray pack, which enables you to mix your own colors or create your own trick paints not available in conventional aerosol cans.

Spray packs also work as effectively and in the same fashion as aerosol cans. With spray packs, you have the advantage of premixing your own colors or using lacquers or "trick" paints that are not available in precanned aerosols.

Aerosols and spray packs are easy to use. Just shake the can vigorously, then spray the paint on, laying smooth, even, overlapping coats over the bike part. Hold the can or pack about a foot away from the surface, keeping each pass an equal distance from the surface.

Spray gun The accepted mainstay tool of the custom painter in the automotive as well as motorcycle field is the spray gun (Fig. 6-2). The spray gun will give the best finish and allow quick, precise coverage of all surface areas.

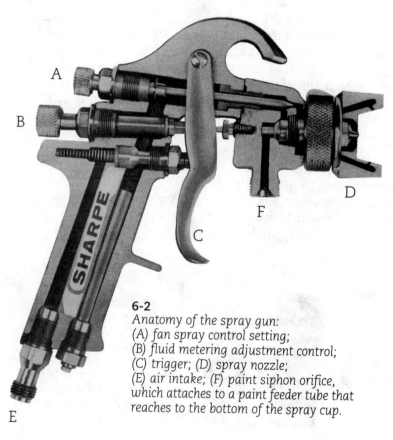

6-2
Anatomy of the spray gun:
(A) fan spray control setting;
(B) fluid metering adjustment control;
(C) trigger; (D) spray nozzle;
(E) air intake; (F) paint siphon orifice,
which attaches to a paint feeder tube that
reaches to the bottom of the spray cup.

The gun most used by painters is the siphon-cup spray gun. It siphons paint out of the cup by means of air pressure, which draws up the fluid through the feeder tube and through the nozzle. Atomization and paint density are metered by external controls and a trigger that is finger-operated.

As the paint is atomized and sprayed through the nozzle, it forms a fan-shaped pattern. An adjustable fan spray valve controls the width of the spray from a small circle to a wide, oval pattern. The small circle concentration works well for small detailing and shading, while the large oval coverage is preferred for overall paint film coating and clearing. Another fluid needle control regulates the volume of paint passing through the nozzle. When painting, spraying and atomization are controlled by pulling back on the trigger.

You'll need to practice and experiment with these adjustments before attempting to paint your bike to avoid dry spray or runs in the paint film. After mastering the adjustment procedure, you should be able to attain a good oval fan spray that when sprayed about 8 to 10 inches from a surface will measure the same distance from top to bottom, which provides maximum spray coverage.

Air pressure must also be carefully set to provide smooth paint film coverage. If too little pressure is used, the mixture will not atomize properly; too much pressure will promote dry spray. To properly regulate air pressure, install a regulator at the compressor or a smaller gun gauge/regulator at the spray-gun handle air intake (Fig. 6-3).

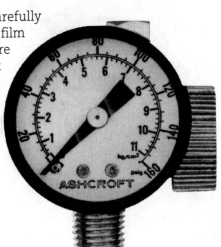

6-3
A regulator such as this, which screws into the air intake, is necessary to control and set pressures at the gun.

A good spray gun such as the Sharpe 75 (or the newer Sharpe 775) will spray all lacquers, enamels, and "trick" paints efficiently. Motorcycle parts are small enough to be suspended by wire or other material in order to paint them. When spraying, keep the gun in motion during each pass at an equal distance to the surface (Fig. 6-4). Eight to 10 inches is a good gun-to-surface distance for spraying good, wet base coats and clear coats.

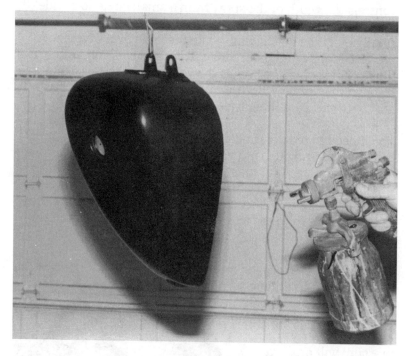

6-4
Motorcycle parts are best sprayed by hanging on a wire or other material so you can cover all the surface areas. Spray parts holding the gun about 8 to 10 inches from the surfaces in an even motion.

Touch-up gun　The touch-up or jamb gun is used by automotive painters for small-area coverage such as doorjambs and confined recesses (Fig. 6-5). For fine shading and detailing it is unexcelled for graphics work, bridging the gap between the spray gun and airbrush. Smaller than the conventional spray gun, the touch-up gun has the identical fan spray and fluid metering controls as its larger counterpart (Fig. 6-6). Refined touch-up guns such as the Badger 400, made by Badger Airbrush Corporation, have optional interchangeable air caps and needles for regular or

6-5
The touchup gun is great for small areas or fine detail. This unit is the Badger 400, available with three cap and needle options for regular or fine detailing.

6-6
Here's an example of finely executed graphics by Jack Thomas, using the Badger 400 touchup gun. All graphics were tape masked.

extra-fine work. I recommend the extra-fine needle and cap for detailing versatility.

Airbrush The airbrush is the most refined, most delicate of spray tools. It is an artist's tool, primarily designed for use in commercial art and photography, but it is equally useful in custom painting for detailing and fine mural work (Fig. 6-7). The airbrushes best suited for custom murals and detailing that will work efficiently with acrylic lacquers are the Badger 150 and 200, Paasche VL-5, DeVilbiss Aerograph Sprite Major, and Iwata HP-C.

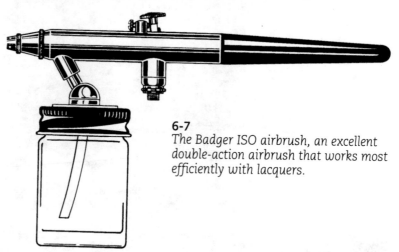

6-7
The Badger ISO airbrush, an excellent double-action airbrush that works most efficiently with lacquers.

There are two types of airbrushes on the market: single-action and double-action. The single-action airbrush emits air and paint in an atomized state as the trigger is depressed (Fig. 6-8). Spray width and paint volume are usually controlled by a knob at the rear of the handle, as shown in the Badger 200 cutaway.

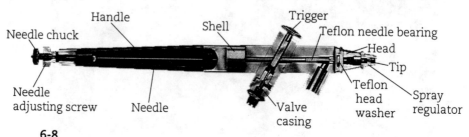

6-8
This Badger 200 airbrush is simpler and easier to use. Its single-action unit must be preset using the exterior needle adjustment screw at the rear of the handle.

The dual-action or double action airbrush is a bit more exacting and versatile than the single-action unit (Fig. 6-9). The term "double action" connotates the method by which the airbrush is triggered and the paint and air atomized. Depressing the button controls the airflow; sliding the button back (the button is linked to the paint flow needle) controls fluid metering. The more the needle is retracted, the more the paint flows and the larger the spray width.

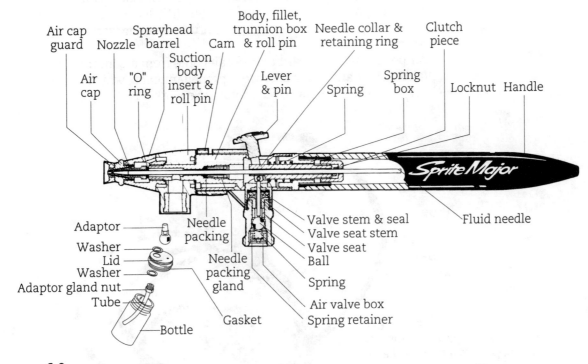

6-9
A cutaway view of the workings of a typical double-action airbrush. The model illustrated is the DeVilbiss Aerograph Sprite Major.

Lacquers will airbrush well, provided care and proper thinning procedures are exercised throughout operation. Since the needle spray orifices of all airbrushes are so minute, they are prone to blocking and clogging, as the lacquers used in bike graphics and murals are fast-drying, highly coagulative liquids. To work properly in airbrushes, lacquer paints (or acrylic enamels) must be thinned out to a great degree. A good working ratio is four parts thinner to one part paint, for starters. This might be a little thin, but safe to work with and good for fine detail work. I prefer a 3:1 ratio.

Good airbrush maintenance is critical to the operation of the tool. The needle orifice must be kept scrupulously clean to enable the airbrush to spray evenly without spitting. Between procedures or when changing colors, the airbrush should be flushed with straight thinner. Medium-drying thinners (Ditzler DTL-876 or equivalent) are recommended for airbrush detailing work.

Air power supply for airbrushes can come from a compressor (airbrush or automotive) or from propellant cans, which can be very efficient for small-area motorcycle work (Fig. 6-10).

6-10
Aerosol packs designed for airbrushes can be used to air-power the tiny utensils. This is a Frisk-Air Propellant pack with a built-in on-off valve.

Proper maintenance is another crucial factor in airbrushing. After use, the needle should be removed, as well as the spray nozzle and head, and immersed in thinner to remove paint buildup (Fig. 6-11). To learn how to properly operate and maintain each individual airbrush, you should consult the operation manual supplied with the unit. Further on in this chapter you will learn some of the various "trick" effects that you can achieve with the airbrush (Fig. 6-12).

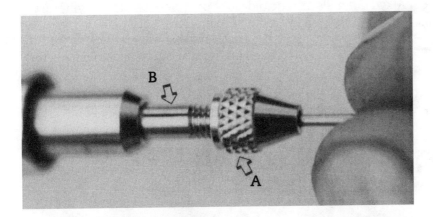

6-11
To remove the needle for cleaning, loosen the needle lock collet (A). The sliding shank (B) should be oiled frequently so that the needle slider valve will work more efficiently.

6-12
Airbrush muralwork on a custom Sportster tank. An airbrush is essential for producing fine detail such as this.

Paint finishing systems

Refinishing systems for motorcycles fall into three categories or types, varying in degree and characteristics. When choosing a system, follow through, using one brand and type of paint throughout. You can deviate only in cases where, for instance, a urethane or acrylic enamel clear coat is used over a compatible lacquer system. Intermixing of brand names or generic substitution is for the most part not recommended.

Synthetic enamels

Alkyd enamels are the oldest of paint media. Slow-drying, slow-curing, prone-to-scratching enamels are not favored today. Their slow-drying characteristic makes them prone to running and sagging when sprayed on heavily, and to picking up dirt in the air.

Acrylic lacquer

Acrylic lacquer is the old standby for bike painters. It is preferred for its quick-drying characteristic, which enables you to tape over it quickly for applying design graphics, stripes, overlays, or murals (Fig. 6-13). Acrylic lacquers are quite durable and weather-resistant, and have excellent color and gloss retention.

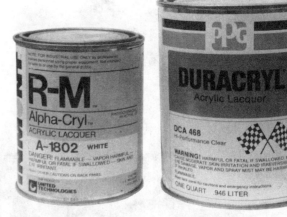

6-13
Two good lacquer systems are the Duracryl and Alpha-Cryl. The former is manufactured by Ditzler, the latter by Rinshed-Mason.

Because weather conditions such as heat and humidity can offset application and finish, a good working knowledge of various thinners and retarders required for lacquer painting is mandatory to obtain optimum results.

Check with your paint supplier for the correct paint-to-thinner ratio, and *never* paint with lacquer on humid, rainy days. If temperature and humidity conditions are not compensated for, problems such as blushing, chalking, sand-scratch swelling, poor adhesion, and color match can occur. Lacquer manufacturers offer fast, medium, slow, and extra-slow-drying thinning agents. They also provide retarders that, when added to the paint solution, slow down drying time to increase gloss, eliminate blushing, and improve flowout to achieve a smoother paint film.

Acrylic enamels and urethanes, the most modern of paints, are said to combine features of alkyd enamel and lacquer (Fig. 6-14). These paints will dry quicker than synthetic enamels but not as rapidly as lacquers. They will dry to high gloss and offer maximum durability and resistance to the elements. They must also be catalyzed prior to use in order to dry and harden properly. Because of their slow-drying characteristic, they are not preferred for design graphics and certainly not muralwork. They are, however, excellent for one-color coating. Some thick urethane paints, which will aid in glamorizing motorcycle finishes, are also offered by such sources as Kosmoski's House of Kolor.

Acrylic enamels & urethanes

6-14
Urethane pearls by Kosmoski's House of Kolor are excellent, vibrant, and highly recommended for one-color pearl coatings.

Urethane clears are popular for overcoating lacquer designs and mural paintwork. They offer optimum gloss and wear-resistant finishes. My favorite formula is to use Ditzler lacquers for base and design work. I clear-coat with Ditzler DAV-75 catalyzed with Ditzler DXR-80. Three full coats provide a fabulous finish that protects the artwork.

Preparation for painting

Prior to paint and design work, some initial preparation must take place. If you are painting over bare metal, the metal must be cleaned and all rust removed with a metal prep solution or sandblasting. The bare metal must then be primed (Fig. 6-15). Some good primers are Ko-901 Ko-Seal, Ditzler Primer 32, and R-M ATS-423. All are good universal primers that can be used under enamels or lacquers.

6-15
Bare metal components must be primed prior to painting. I like and use the Kustom Kolor Ko-Seal, preferably the light grey.

If you are going to do design or mural work on an existing factory finish, retaining the original base color, the procedure is a little different. First scuff the entire component with a 3M scuff pad until the surface is dulled (Fig. 6-16). Then apply an adhesion sealer if you are painting lacquer over a catalyzed acrylic enamel. If you are painting over a lacquer finish, you need only to scuff the surface.

Masking

Design motifs and graphics must be masked. A popular choice is automotive-grade masking tape. The thinner widths can be used to lay out designs and negotiate curves, the wider widths to fill in. Or you can use masking paper, wrapping paper, or newspaper for large-area masking (Fig. 6-17).

6-17
Tape can be used for masking large areas covered with masking paper, wrapping paper, or newspaper; the two former are preferred.

Spray mask Liquid spray mask is an excellent masking medium and one I prefer. As discussed previously, it is a viscous liquid manufactured by Metalflake Corp. that is sprayed on with a spray gun. It dries to a rubbery film that can be cut. Intricate designs can be created with this easy-to-apply medium, which is water-soluble and thinnable (Figs. 6-18, 6-19).

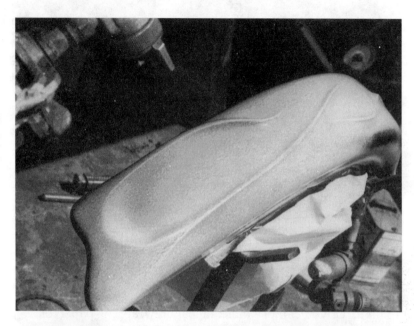

6-18
Spray mask is applied with a production gun in two heavy coats. While wet, the spray mask remains opaque.

6-19
As the spray mask dries it becomes translucent, drying to a tough, rubbery film. It cuts easily with an X-acto knife or razor blade.

Trick paints

There are many trick paints and procedures used in bike customizing—some instituted by the distinctive paints themselves, some by the use of spray gun, airbrush, stencil, and other methods. This section will cover some of the popular approaches used today for graphic enhancement. Virtually all trick paints are marketed as acrylic lacquers.

Candies

Candies, considered by some the most alluring of trick paints, are nothing more than basic translucent toners. They are usually painted over silver, metallic, or light-colored base coats, the color density built up as consecutive coats are applied. Candies are not sprayed on in the same manner as opaque color coats. They are hazed on in thin, even, light coats until the desired color effect is achieved.

The drawback of candies is that they show dirt or dust that has gotten into the paint film during application, and such flaws continue to show through consecutive coats. Candy coats cannot be touched up. If they are flawed or damaged, they must be repainted. Painting with candies is not recommended for the novice; it takes a lot of time and practice to master candy coating.

Pearls

Pearls, among the most exotic of custom finishes, are easily spotted by their pearl-like luster. They are semiopaque, iridescent paints and are generally applied, like candies, over a base or ground coat that may be of a similar or contrasting color for enhancing the finished effect. Popular pearl base coats are white, black, and silver. If a solid pearl look is required, a base coat of a hue similar to the pearlescent color is advised.

Pearlescents should be administered with caution, in consecutive mist coats with adequate flashing time in between. Topcoating with acrylic lacquer or clear acrylic enamel is strongly advised, as pearls can easily scratch if not clear-coated.

Murano pearls

Easily recognized by their flip-flop reflective appearance when viewed at different angles, Murano pearls are extremely transparent. Base coats will show through almost unaffected when viewed at a direct ninety-degree angle. At other angles, they give off a pearly hue of their own.

Pearls are available in pastes to mix with lacquer or enamel clears, or come in premixed ready-to-spray consistency from Metalflake. The Metalflake Muranos are labeled Flip-Flop. Some exciting Murano pearl offerings are also available from Aerolac and Kosmoski's House of Kolor.

Muranos, like pearls and candies, must be mist-coated, building up to the desired density.

Neon   Dayglo colors are also available for that wild look. The best offerings are from Kosmoski's House of Kolor. They are of a urethane base and must be clear-coated with a gloss topcoat, as neon or Dayglo colors give off a matte finish when not clear-coated.

Eerie Dess   Eerie Dess, so named because of the eerie iridescent effect it produces, is an easy paint to apply and is slow-drying so that it can be worked in applique fashion.

The area to be painted is masked off (Fig. 6-20). Then the Eerie Dess solution is sprayed on wet in the same manner as base coating. Finally, wrinkled Saran Wrap is dabbed all over the Eerie Dessed panel (Fig. 6-21). In the example, you can see the effect achieved with this simple process (Figs. 6-22, 6-23).

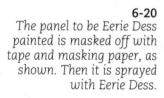

6-20
The panel to be Eerie Dess painted is masked off with tape and masking paper, as shown. Then it is sprayed with Eerie Dess.

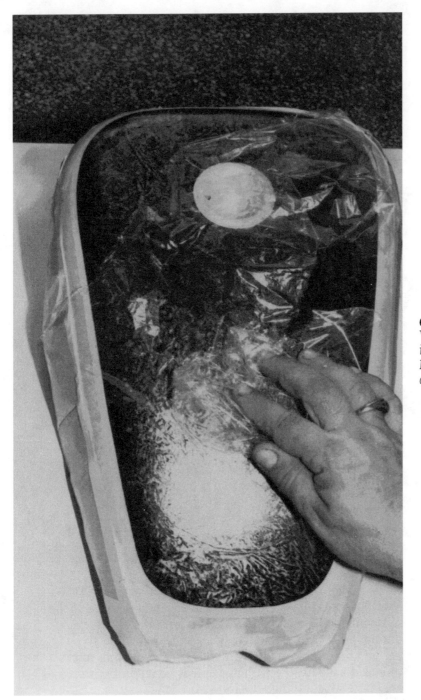

6-21
While still wet, Saran Wrap
is applied to the Eerie Dess.
It is laid on and dabbed in
applique fashion.

6-22
Close-up view of a typical Eerie Dess motif. Eerie Dess must be clear-coated for permanence.

6-23
Another example of Eerie Dess paneling. This is a currently popular design medium.

Metalflake

Heavy flake coatings were extremely popular in the 1950s and '60s, but metalflake's popularity has waned in favor of the more intriguing candy, pearl, and other optical-art finishes that are not as garish—although every once in a while you will come across an all-metalflake painted bike. Today, finer micro flakes are used, dispersed sparingly in clear-coat solutions to give some metallic highlights (Fig. 6-24).

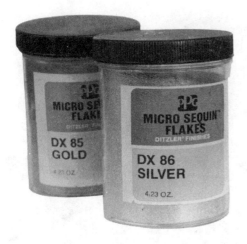

6-24
Metalflake is available from Ditzler in fine particles. Metalflake Corp. also makes flake in micro, regular, and extra-large particles.

In metalflake painting, the flakes replace the pigment common to ordinary paint and are suspended in a solution of clear lacquer. For overall flake coverage, about four ounces of flake are mixed into a quart of dilute, ready-to-spray clear coat. The solution is sprayed through a production spray gun, resulting in a deep layer of clear-coat saturated with flake particles. Pressure at the gun should be about 25 psi to allow the flakes to adhere flat to the surface. Pressures exceeding 25 psi can cause some flakes to bounce off the surface or stick sideways and not lay flat. To keep the flakes in proper suspension in the clear coat, the gun should be constantly agitated and preferably shaken before each spray pass.

Design techniques

A number of design techniques have become standard through the years and quite popular when used in paint schemes or in graphic art paneling.

Cobwebbing

Cobwebbing is simple to apply. It is achieved by using lacquer undiluted, straight from the paint can. Since the paint is unthinned, it will blow and scatter over the surface in thready, cobweblike patterns (Fig. 6-25). The higher the spray pressure used, the more prominent and dense the cobwebbing will appear.

Cobwebbing must be clear-coated with at least five coats to be properly contained in the undercoat. After four coats, the cobwebbed area should be wet-sanded with 400 grit paper to

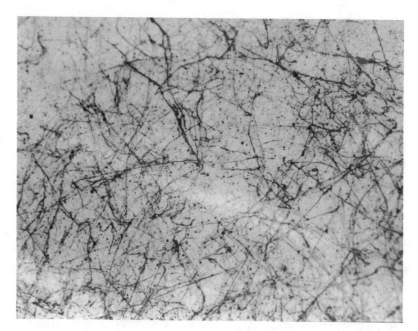

6-25
A cobweb pattern.
Cobwebbing is distinctive,
unique, and easy to apply.

even out the pronounced thread irregularities. One final clear coat evens out the paint film.

Fish scaling

Fish scaling is another eye-catching design effect and is usually undertaken with an airbrush, though it can also be achieved with a touch-up gun at its finest setting. A stencil is made using round stick-on labels aligned on a straightedge (Fig. 6-26A). The stencil is laid across the surface and the edge is airbrushed. At each consecutive pass, the stencil is aligned with each preceding scale line, centered on the hemisphere of the next line to be rendered, as shown (Fig. 6-26B). The scaling procedure is continued until the panel or masked area is fully scaled (Fig. 6-26C).

Stencil overlays

Op-art patterns can be created using stencils precut from file-folder stock or Bristol board. The patterns are transferred with the airbrush as the stencil overlaps each preceding stenciled segment (Fig. 6-27). Some novel design effects can be realized using the stencil overlays method (Fig. 6-28).

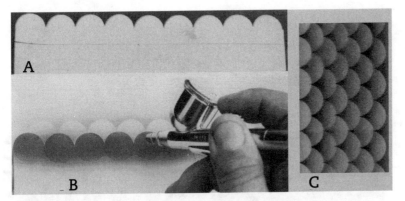

6-26
Fish scaling. (A) shows the stencil fabricated for scaling. In (B) you can see how consecutive coats build up the scale pattern. (C) shows a typical fish-scale pattern.

6-27
A stencil is cut from file-folder stock and used in an overlay fashion to execute an op-art design motif.

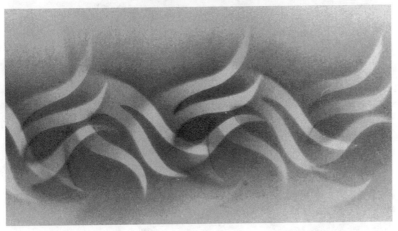

6-28
The complete design pattern executed with the overlay method. Design shape possiblities are unlimited.

Lace painting

Again you use the airbrush to create the design, this time with lace as the stencil patterning medium. The lace is placed tightly against the surface and airbrushed (Fig. 6-29). Use light, consecutive strokes, building up the color slowly. Do not allow the lace to become saturated with paint or it will stick to the undercoat and, when pulled off, will pull off the undercoat (Fig. 6-30).

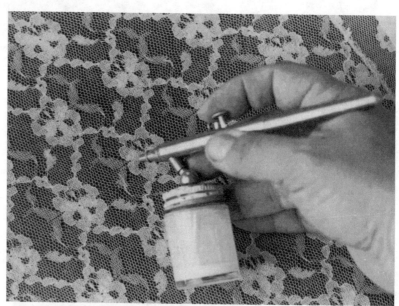

6-29
Lace is stretched over the surface to serve as a design stencil. Then the airbrush fills in and transfers the lace pattern to the surface.

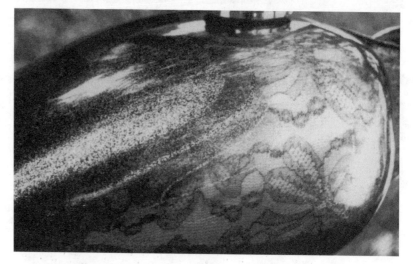

6-30
Here's a tank exhibiting a transferred lace pattern. An infinite variety of laces are available at material goods and fabric stores.

Flames are another throwback to the '50s era, but are still popular today in motorcycle paint schemes (Fig. 6-31).

Flames can be laid out and masked off, but I prefer to use spray mask. After the film is fully dry, I lay out the pattern with a grease pencil, then cut out the flame and peel off the spray mask (Fig. 6-32). I then paint on the flames using an airbrush (Fig. 6-33).

Flames

6-31
This is an excellent example of a flame pattern, exhibited on Joe Ferraro's Harley. Note the fine designwork and symmetry.

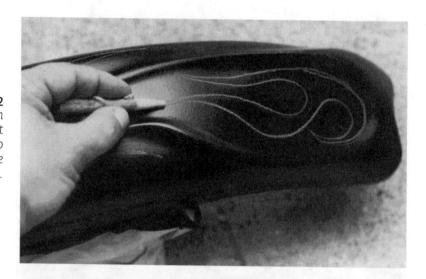

6-32
A flame pattern is laid out on the spray mask film. Then it is cut out with an X-acto knife, baring the area to be painted.

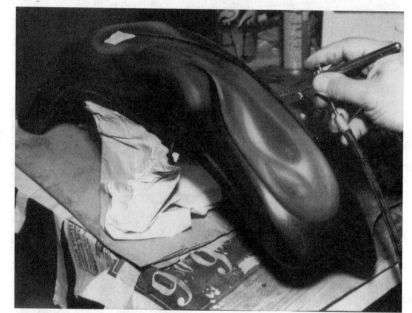

6-33
The flames are then airbrushed in. When the outlying spray mask is peeled off, the flame pattern will be revealed.

Freak drops

"Freak drops" are another op-art design effect that can be done easily with the airbrush (Fig. 6-34). Blobs of color are blown onto the surface with the airbrush and before each paint blob dries, air from the airbrush is blown into the center of each blob, allowing it to spread out in spidery tentacles. Some

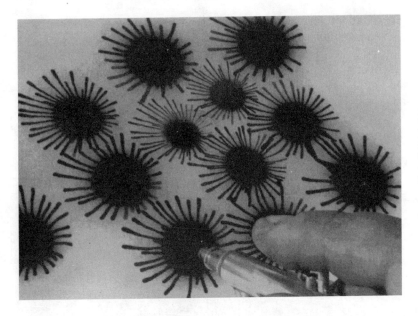

6-34
Freak drop patterns. Blobs of paint are deposited on the surface, then fanned out to produce the design patterns illustrated. Air is used to dispel the paint into tentacle-encircled forms.

interesting effects can be achieved, especially with multicolored candy freak drops overlapping each other.

Murals

Murals can be created freehand, with the aid of masks and stencils, or by combining both methods. The airbrush is the primary tool used, since it is the only spray tool that can produce fine, exacting detail.

In the color section, a step-by-step mural approach shows how to apply hand and stencil work on a custom tank (Fig. 6-35).

6-35
A detailed mural created by airbrush and some hand detailing. The pearl ribbon motif was laid out with tape, masked, then filled in with a touch-up gun.

Airbrush templates The Badger Airbrush Corporation offers a number of various-sized circular and elliptical templates (Fig. 6-36). These can prove useful for creating op-art and overlay designs with the airbrush.

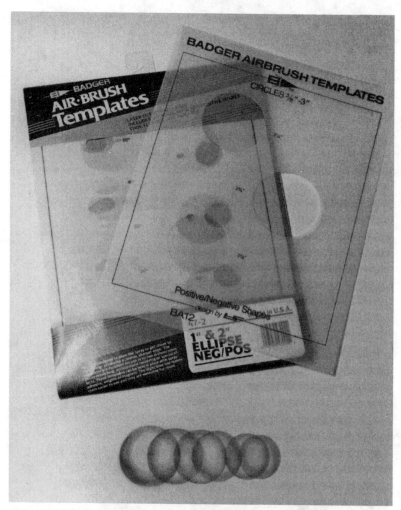

6-36
Airbrush templates available from Badger Airbrush Corp. can be used for op-art overlay patterns. At the bottom is an example using graduated circles.

The custom painting techniques presented in this chapter—as all the projects in this book—are within the reach of the novice customizer. Broken down into simple steps, the jobs are not overly difficult to tackle. If you follow the instructions, you too can enhance your motorcycle with custom decor. For those of you who wish to consider other custom approaches, I recommend another of my books, *The Art of Custom Painting,* published by Metalflake. Another book for recommended reading is *Airbrush Techniques for Custom Painting,* published by the Badger Airbrush Corporation and available direct from Badger or at most art supply stores.

Powder coating

Powder coating is a new name for a process discovered years ago called electrostatic painting. Powder coat is not paint *per se,* but when applied becomes a film coating twice as durable as liquid paints and impervious to chipping and flaking. When baked and cured, powder coating can withstand five times the impact of paint, has triple the longevity of paint, and is highly fade- and corrosion-resistant. In addition, powder-coated parts can be mounted, ready to weather the elements, one hour after coating. The high resiliency factor of this medium makes it ideal for painting such motorcycle components as tanks, fenders, and frames in particular, and cast wheels.

In powder coating, the color or pigment is shot out of a special gun in powder form, dry. The gun contains a positive electrical charge and dispenses the powder onto the part to be coated, which is grounded (negative). Since negative attracts positive, the powder is drawn to the grounded metal piece and adheres to the surface (Fig. 6-37). The powder-coated part is then inserted into a heating oven or compartment, which heats the

6-37
The coating process is carried out in a special booth. Charged particles of powder are attracted to the electrically grounded part.

part to a point where the powder coat cures. As the temperature rises, the fusion of powder to metal surface takes place (Fig. 6-38). The curing process takes place within the special oven which bakes the coating on at 400 degrees Fahrenheit for about half an hour.

6-38
Baking in a special high-heat oven fuses the paint coating to the metal, resulting in a most durable, resilient color film.

When fully cured, the powder-coated object attains a high-gloss finish and after cooling can be mounted dry. The curing (drying) time is minimal, since no liquid solvents are involved. Since the coating is never wet, it cannot run or sag. The dry, electrostatically attracted powder also coats evenly, reaching into all corners and crevices.

Another benefit of powder coating is that there is no overspray or waste, toxic or otherwise. Excess powder that does not adhere to the metal can be collected and refiltered for later use.

Powder coatings are marketed in smooth or textured versions. The smooth coatings are available in metallic and clear versions, as well as an infinite variety of base coat colors. Varied effects can be achieved by multi-color coating, spraying on metallics for candy effects. Powder coatings can also be applied over chromed or polished metal surfaces.

What makes this paint so popular and conducive to engine component painting is its durability; it won't chip, crack, or peel and is impervious to weather, moisture, and engine heat, retaining its color under all conditions.

One of the foremost leaders in powder coating is Sumax, also known for their fine motorcycle accessories. Sumax will powder-coat any part or automotive component in one of many dazzling solid, glossy or matte, or even candy colors on request. The Sumax powder coating facilities are designed to accept and coat all parts, from small caps to large frames. For more information on Sumax powder coating, send for Sumax's free brochure and price list. Just write to:

Sumax
337 Clear Rd.
Oriskany, New York 13424

CHAPTER 7

Engine performance modifications

THOUGH CUSTOM Harleys are built mainly with an eye towards design, many Harley buffs concern themselves with performance upgrading packages. In this chapter we will cover some of the most popular engine upgrading accessories and procedures—some basic, some more sophisticated. The key to optimum performance and top engine efficiency is the proper combination of quality parts that work in unison rather than against each other. Some of you might want a basic, simple performance boost that can be realized by the simple addition of an aftermarket "heavy breathing" carburetor; others may want to go the more radical rebuild route. This chapter will familiarize you with the more popular alternatives.

Carburetors

Though stock carburetion on most contemporary Harleys is more stable and sophisticated than older Linkert, Bendix, and Tillotson components, there are a few specialized aftermarket carburetors with optimum design characteristics that outperform the standard equipment. Here we present the tops in "heavy breathers" that will guarantee performance excellence when mounted on any Harley engine, old or new.

The S & S Super E

S & S has established itself as a leader for decades in Harley carburetion. Their newest Super E is considered by some as incomparable in terms of performance efficiency (Figs. 7-1, 7-2).

The new Super E features welcome improvements over previous models that make it ideal for upgrading performance on the newer Evolution motors. This carburetor is also well suited for providing optimum performance on all Shovelhead engines up to 1984.

A main feature of the "Shorty" is the inclusion of an accelerator pump, which greatly improves throttle response at lower rpm

and assists in cold starts. Riders who like instant, positive acceleration will appreciate the immediate throttle response achieved by injecting fuel directly into the venturi as the throttle is opened. The Super E also relies on an enrichener as opposed to a conventional choke; more than adequate for cold starts, it also provides faster idling for smooth warmups. About an inch and a half shorter than prior S & S models, the Super E provides optimum airflow.

The S & S kit is complete and even includes an extended piece of vacuum hose for connecting the S & S manifold (Fig 7-3) to Harley's vacuum advance switch. Most Harleys featuring a

dual-cable pull-open throttle will find all the necessary hardware in the kit. Harleys fitted with single-cable throttle advance will require suitable modification hardware, which is also available from S & S.

Tuning the Super E is simplicity itself. S & S has gone to great lengths to design the carburetor so that it can be easily tuned by the average rider. S & S also offers the carb pre-tuned for the desired customer application; just provide S & S with the proper setup specifications of your particular engine and they will pre-jet the unit according to your needs.

Engine performance modifications 169

7-3
*Evolution S & S manifolds
come complete with all
bolt-on accessory components
and hardware.*

The S & S Super E contains three fuel circuits that should be finely adjusted: idle, intermediate, and main. The carb should give great performance right out of the box if you have provided the proper information for your particular engine requirements. A little tip: Even if the carb provides good performance out of the box, adjust the accelerator pump and try alternate jets; experiment to obtain the best horsepower and mileage combo. The S & S must be fine-tuned to deliver maximum performance and no carburetor is simpler to tune than the Super E. The expansive installation and jetting instructions provided by S & S (it's a mini-manual) will give you infinite guidance in preparing the carburetor for foolproof operation.

The 40mm Dell'Orto

Marketed and pioneered by Rivera Engineering, Whittier, California, 40mm Dell'Orto dual throat carburetor kits are available for Sportsters and Big Twins up to 1984 and for all Evolution Big Twin and Sportster engines (Fig. 7-4). The kits for Sportsters and Big Twins up to 1984 will fit models mounting 3½ gallon or custom tanks, differing only in the choice of various manifolds. All manifolds are available in stroker sizes. The kits include velocity stacks, choice of air cleaners, necessary hardware, and full tuning instructions. Push-pull brackets are also available if required. When ordering a kit for

7-4
The 40mm Dell'Orto is as massive as it is powerful—a standout physically and performance-wise.

7-5
Special Dell'Orto kits are available from Rivera Engineering for virtually all Harley engine applications.

Engine performance modifications **171**

older engines, you must specify the year of the machine, size of gas tanks, and air cleaner choice (Fig. 7-5).

For Evolution Big Twins and Evolution Sportsters, Rivera offers a new manifold designed to be used on five gallon tanks, with a push-pull boss cast onto the manifold itself. All kits feature bolt-on mounting and a choice of air cleaners. Carburetors will be pre-jetted according to specifications that must be supplied by the customer.

Labeled by experts as the next best thing to fuel injection, the Dell'Orto offers optimum performance when installed on Harley engines. This "juice gooser" is capable of producing results more favorable than most carburetors, even those specially designed for Harley-Davidson engines. The 40mm series carburetor is of the downdraft (or, in the case of Harleys sidedraft) type. This is a two-barrel carb with dual synchromesh throttles that work in unison. Among the sophisticated features of the Dell'Orto is air-bleed correction, which is governed by its internal emulsion tubes, refined jets that work in conjunction with various other jets, and a spray feeder tube that emits a finely metered, vaporized fuel mixture into the auxiliary venturi, then the main venturi.

A number of air jets and emulsion tubes are available for rejetting and fine-tuning the carburetor. There are over a dozen emulsion tubes and idle speed jets that in various combinations allow nearly infinite tuning. The main advantage of automatic corrective bleeding action is better atomization of fuel, since the spray tube feeding into the venturi supplies not only gasoline (as in the case of a simple spray carburetor) but also a suitably proportioned fuel-air mixture. By incorporating emulsion tube and idle tube combos, fuel supply curves can be further corrected, affording the best possible mixture metering for proper engine feed. Utilizing the sophisticated rejetting system and combinations, the recommended combo for stock Shovelhead and Evolution engines, according to Rivera, is a #5 Emulsion tube coupled with a #1 idle jet (Fig. 7-6). The Dell'Orto carburetor tends to stick out more than most aftermarket carbs, but this slight drawback is well worth the performance gain realized.

7-6
Looking into the dual throats of the Dell'Orto we can see the main venturi and the auxiliary or secondary venturi which are removable and can be interchanged with varied auxiliary venturi to modify carburetor performance.

SU carburetors

The SU carburetor goes back several years and was at one time the forerunner of all vacuum-type carburetors. It was designed as an automotive carburetor and was stock equipment on Jaguars, Austin-Healeys, Triumphs, MGs, and Volvos (Fig. 7-7).

7-7
Rivera's Eliminator II SU mounted on an older Panhead engine.

SU models with 1½-inch throat diameters are best suited for Knuckleheads, Panheads, Shovelheads, and new Evolutions. Proper adapting manifolds must be used to mount SUs and they are readily available from suppliers such as Rivera Engineering and Drag Specialties (Fig. 7-8). Specially designed upswept one-piece manifolds are also designed by Rivera for the 80-cubic inch Evolution and 1966–84 Shovelheads as well as older Harley engine versions. Drag Specialties and Rivera also offer specially modified SUs for Shovelheads and Evolutions.

7-8
Shown here is an older S U with special adaptor manifold for the older Harley Panhead engine.

The SU Eliminator I is available for FL, FX, and XL Harley-Davidson engines. Another model, the SU Eliminator II, is marketed specifically for use with 1984–89 Evolution engines. A special upswept manifold allows tucking in the carburetor closer to the engine; SUs tend to stick out when mounted on some Shovelheads, Panheads, and Knuckleheads. Eliminator I and II kits come complete with manifold, air cleaner, gasket, and mounting hardware.

The SU is a constant-velocity, vacuum-type carburetor incorporating a variable venturi. The throat slide connected to the fuel-metering needle is vacuum-controlled, automatically adjusting fuel flow and ingestion according to the requirements of the engine. Volumetric gas intake is automatically controlled by means of a vacuum diaphragm. Throttle response is immediate with no annoying lag—you can whip the throttle full-on, yet the engine will take on fuel only as fast as it can use it. Acceleration is even and precise. Though accessory jets are available, manipulating and resetting the stock needle usually will suffice for fine-tuning the carb.

Minor maintenance is required to keep the SU functioning properly. Since the idle vacuum diaphragm is oil-damped, an inner chamber containing transmission fluid necessary for damping must be kept filled.

It has been proven that with the addition of an SU carburetor, an 8 to 10 horsepower increase can be immediately realized. Of all the add-on aftermarket carbs, the SU provides, in my estimation, the best mid-range performance and best gas mileage on all Harley engines.

Mikuni HS-40

The Mikuni 40mm smoothbore carburetor is another high-efficiency car-designed carburetor for the new Evolution engines; it will bolt on directly to the Evolution manifold or can be used with the Ram Jett 80 Evolution manifolds (Fig. 7-9). (See Appendix for Ram Jett listing.)

7-9
The Mikuni HS-40 is another high-efficiency carburetor. Here it is shown with its included manifold mount and choke assembly.
The HF-40 performance characteristics make it ideal for the new Evolution motors.

7-10
*Inside view of a Mikuni,
showing the large 40 mm
throat and large venturi
chamber. The fuel jet can
also be seen midway into
the throat.*

The kit comes complete with carburetor, choke and throttle cables, adapters, and clamps. The Mikuni HS-40 features a high-flowing, 40mm smoothbore venturi and an adjustable accelerator pump for improved throttle response. It is unusually versatile in the respect that it will provide correct fuel mixtures for engines with differing tuning setups without modification (Fig. 7-10).

The HS series carburetors require a push-pull throttle-cable assembly to ensure positive closing of the throttle valve. High vacuums created or dirt ingested (if low-restriction air filters are used) can inhibit the throttle valve from closing quickly, so a good, strong push-pull assembly is mandatory.

The Mikuni HS-40 carburetor is a bolt-on item and is properly jetted for the stock Evolution engines. Major engine modifications including high compression and racing cams may require minor tuning adjustments. The HS-40's sensitivity to engine fuel requirements allows its use in most applications, so it comes correctly jetted.

The idle circuit supplies fuel at idling speed, influencing fuel flow up to ¼ throttle. Three tunable parts constitute this circuit. The pilot jet controls maximum flow through the idle circuit. The pilot air jet controls air volume that mixes with fuel from the pilot jet. When this mixes with the pilot jet fuel, it creates a fuel-air froth that traverses the idle circuit passages more rapidly than fuel alone would. The pilot screw governs how much of the circuit's vaporized fuel mixture is allowed to enter the carburetor venturi. A pilot adjustment screw controls idle mixture.

Idle circuit can be adjusted by changing either pilot or pilot air jets. Installing a one-size-larger pilot jet will give nearly the same effect as a one-size-smaller air jet. The air jet is easier to change, as it is more accessible than the pilot jet. The larger the pilot air jet, the leaner the mixture; the smaller the pilot air jet, the richer the mixture. After changing either the pilot or the pilot air jet, it is necessary to readjust the pilot screw for optimum idling.

The main system provides fuel between $\frac{1}{16}$ and full throttle, whereas the idle circuit provides most fuel near $\frac{1}{16}$ throttle. The main system takes over and becomes the predominant mixture controller from about $\frac{1}{4}$ throttle.

The main system features three tunable segments. The needle jet controls mixture from $\frac{1}{16}$ to about $\frac{1}{4}$ throttle. The needle itself controls $\frac{1}{4}$ to $\frac{3}{4}$ throttle mixtures. The main jet controls the mixture between $\frac{3}{4}$ and full throttle.

The needle contains both an even and a tapered section. The combination of needle jet diameter and needle diameter create the opening through which all main system fuel flows. At $\frac{1}{4}$ throttle, the even diameter of the needle is within the needle jet wall's main system fuel flow, which is controlled by the needle jet size.

Needle jets are available in various sizes with differing inside diameters. The larger the needle jet, the richer the fuel mixture within the range of operation. The needle can be raised or lowered and set by means of notches at the top of the needle. The raising or lowering of the needle determines at what throttle setting the tapered segment is elevated out from the needle jet.

Fuel flow is determined by the needle taper from where it starts to raise out of the needle jet up to about $\frac{3}{4}$ throttle. Raising or lowering the needle makes the mixture richer or leaner, respectively. At $\frac{3}{4}$ throttle, the enlarged orifice is ample in size so that the main jet takes control of the fuel flow. The taper of the needle has no influence on fuel flow at full throttle.

The Mikuni HS-40 carburetor contains a special accelerator pump that injects fuel into the throat of the carburetor when the throttle is opened. At low rpm, when the throttle is opened, air velocity within the carb drops, pushing out the fuel mixture. Fuel fed from the pump helps maintain a more correct fuel mixture until air velocity reverts to a normal state. Adjustments to the accelerator pump allow fuel to be injected into the carb throat over a wide throttle-opening range. Various-sized pump nozzles will affect the rate of fuel injection. The pump's starting-and-ending-point adjustments regulate total flow volume (Fig. 7-16).

The Mikuni starter system activates when the choke is opened and the throttle is closed. It is a built-in small carburetor designed to provide rich fuel mixtures to facilitate starting, and replaces cruder conventional choke mechanisms. With the throttle opened and the choke knob pulled, air stops flowing through the starter system, which ceases to deliver a rich mixture to the engine. If the engine loads up while the starter system is engaged, it can be cleared by advancing the throttle. The starter system will take effect again when the throttle is shut down.

The starter jet is the sole replaceable component within the starter system. A larger starter jet richens the starter mixture, while a smaller jet leans out the mixture. For normal operation, the use of a 55mm starter jet is recommended.

Other Mikuni carburetors, such as the 36mm and 38mm, are available for FX, FL, and XL Shovelheads up to 1981, or late 1981–89 Harley-Davidson models with single-cable throttle controls.

Stroker engines

By far, the most effective way to increase Harley engine horsepower is by "stroking." What you are really doing when you increase the stroke is building a bigger engine within the confines of the same engine case. The addition of big-bore pistons augments this brute power. Harley engines lend themselves well to both boring and stroking and for this reason one heck of a lot of serious Harley buffs are running around the land with bikes sporting stroker powerplants.

When you build a stroked engine, you increase the "arm" or offset in the crankshaft so that the rod end (and consequently the piston) moves up and down farther on each engine revolution. Lengthening the stroke increases the cubic inch displacement of the engine. Stroking is considered a "bottom end" modification procedure, even though it creates some effect on the top end (pistons, barrels, etc.).

Stroking procedures

To increase crankshaft offset, the crankpin or the bearings that the rods ride on must be relocated farther away from the centerline of the crankshaft (Fig. 7-11). Harley engines feature crankshafts that are built up of individual main shafts, flywheels, and crankpins integrated together. New or reworked flywheels with crankpin holes located "farther out" are the foundation for the stroker bottom end. As a stroking alternative, you can sometimes fit a special offset crankpin (Fig. 7-12) that will achieve the same purpose pressing into stock flywheels incorporating an eccentric bearing surface positioned in the direction of a longer stroke. The best method is restroking the crankshaft, if you have machine shop facilities and expertise, or, ideally, purchasing a restroking kit.

The distance that the offset is moved outwards serves to augment the stroke in two directions: one as the piston rises to top dead center, and one as it falls to bottom dead center. In actuality, stroke is *twice* the total offset from crankshaft centerline, as you can see in Fig. 7-11.

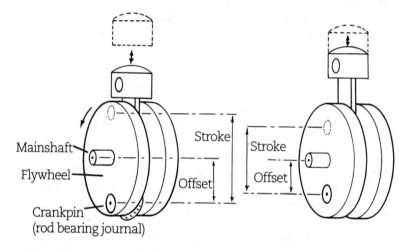

7-11
The difference between a stock and a stroked crankshaft.

With piston travel increased in both directions in an engine designed for a lesser given stroke, you can see the potential for problems. Since the piston domes now rise higher on each revolution of the crank, you will realize some sudden or extreme boost in compression ratio. Piston domes can conflict with valves or the tops of the combustion chambers. On the bottom side of the crank revolution, piston skirts can butt the top faces of the flywheels or bearing retainers.

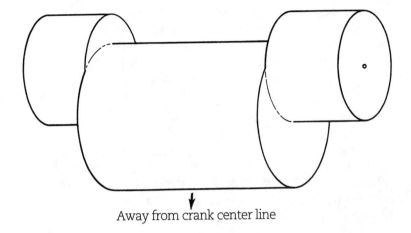

Away from crank center line

7-12
An offset crankpin is a second way to achieve longer stroke—but not as ideal as remachining or replacing the stock crank with stroker flywheels.

There are several ways to compensate for the increased piston travel encountered within the confines of a stroker engine. Fortunately, most " bolt-in" stroker lower end or crank-and-rod kits include specially designed rods that are either shorter than standard or contain lowered wrist pin holes, which inhibit pistons from rising too far from their original desired boundaries. Some flywheel cranks are also produced with lesser diameter than their stock counterparts in order to alleviate bottom fouling problems. Another alternative is the use of "stroker" pistons. These pistons feature a narrower skirt to assist in clearing the tops of the flywheels, and less dome above the wrist pin to counteract the longer travel on top.

The last alternative method is the use of longer aftermarket cylinders or barrels that relocate the cylinder heads back to their original working distance from the piston dome. These "stroker" cylinders can require the insertion of longer pushrods and longer oil feeders. To achieve the same purpose, stroker cylinder base plates can be mounted beneath stock barrels for increasing barrel height and uninhibited piston travel.

All the aforementioned compromises work well for moderately stroked engines. Radical strokers with excessively long strokes can require the notching and relieving of engine cases, cylinder walls, or even the rods themselves to some degree, since longer rods tend to generate radical rod operation angles. The

Engine performance modifications 181

majority of stroker configurations, however, tend to swing more toward conventional than radical extremes. Harley engines of all types, newer or older, are particularly suitable for stroking because very big bore sizes are limited by the close locations of the followers and tappets to the cylinder holes.

Stroker components

The Harley aftermarket abounds in a host of quality stroker components. S & S offers the widest array of ready-made bolt-in stroker kits featuring special forged and balanced flywheels, special rods, and connecting pins. The flywheels can also be purchased alone. Ready-made S & S stroker flywheels are highly recommended for all Harley engines. They are designed to fit into stock engines without too much finagling.

S & S stroker flywheels are machined from heat-treated, closed die steel forgings. This is more costly than using iron alloy castings, but the end results are worth it. The structurally superior parts, upon assembly of the lower end, have been noted for their easy "truing" qualities, a testimony to rigid machining standards and specifications. S & S flywheels are machined for use in all Harley-Davidson OHV Big Twins and Sportsters and can be made to fit "Flathead" Big Twins in some instances. They are available with stock Harley-Davidson mainshaft tapers or with a special S & S design that utilizes a large 6-degree keyed sprocket shaft tapered left flywheel and a conventional tapered right flywheel. The extra large sprocket shaft taper has more shaft-to-flywheel contact area for a better gripping advantage than stock 1971 and earlier style tapers. The 6-degree angle has been found to work best and it makes for easier truing during assembly. And the addition of the key to the left taper, lacking on stock flywheels since 1972, reduces potential sprocket shaft spinning, which has become a problem for drag racers and some engine builders ever since the advent of the keyless left flywheel in stock engines. We recommend the use of the S & S special design flywheels for drag racing in 1970 and later engines or in any application where the engine builder has some doubt as to the strength of the stock combination (Fig. 7-13).

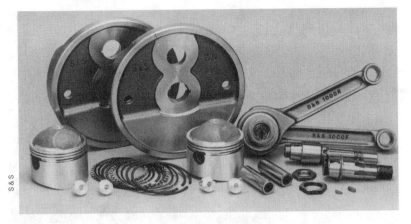

S&S

7-13
Ironhead XL stock bore stroker kits are available in 4⅝" (74"); 4½" (72"); 4⁷⁄₁₆" (71"). Rods and shafts are optional.

As for compensating equipment for Harley-Davidson strokers, there's an assortment of that also: stroker pistons from S & S, MC and Axtell; extended cylinders from Axtell; and even stroker plates from major accessory sources.

Even with some moderate stroke jobs on such engines as the older Sportsters, the position of the oil return holes must be lowered or else oil will be dumped onto the face of the piston above the oil ring, as it travels farther into the bore than before. Axtell markets special stroker cylinders that contain the relocated oil hole and feature prenotched cylinders, cutting down necessary machining steps that must be performed with stroker barrels.

"Top end" modifications can also contribute to substantial power boosting. The aftermarket abounds in Harley top end performance goodies from mild to wild; here are just a few of them.

Top end modifications

Heads are a basic bolt-on item; a number with varying performance capabilities are marketed by Rivera Engineering, S & S, Axtell, Strocieck, and Sputhe. Heads are easily replaced in simple bolt-on application. Upgraded performance heads assure perfect alignment and fitment. Head swaps can be undertaken with the motor either in the bike or on the bench (Fig. 7-14).

High-performance heads

7-14
Rocker boxes and heads are readily accessible and easy to exchange or remove for modification. Here the late Lawrence Pressley, master Harley mechanic, proceeds to do a head job at Heaven on Wheels, Ft. Lauderdale, Florida.

One of the finest replacement head systems is by Strocieck (Fig. 7-15). The Strocieck units are high-performance hemi-heads that are completely ported and polished for optimum gas flow and positive plug firing (Fig. 7-16). They are composed of milled aluminum and are provided with two enlarged intake ports and two oversized exhaust ports. Spark-plug seating is situated dead center between the valves, not offset as in standard Harley items. This modified setup makes possible more even gas firing in the combustion chamber. Implementing Strocieck heads in place of stock Shovelhead heads will result in a 15-hp performance gain.

7-15
High-performance heads: These Strocieck units provide noticeable horsepower gains. They are machine-milled from aluminum.

7-16
Note the mirror-finish chamber dome on a Strocieck head. Chamber surface polishing provides optimum fuel flow within the head chamber and assists engine breathing.

Fueling/Rivera 4-valve heads

The hottest setup in performance is the Fueling/Rivera 4-valve head. Created by leading motorcycle engine researcher/developer Jim Fueling, this breakthrough is distributed and marketed by Rivera Engineering (Fig. 7-17). The magnificent performance package is easy to install and features all the necessary hardware as well as replacement 4-valve heads and special rocker covers. It is highly recommended that the installation be undertaken by one who has more than a basic working knowledge of the Harley-Davidson Evolution Big Twin Engine.

7-17
Fueling/Rivera 4-valve heads were designed for Evolution engines 1984 and up. The Stage I kit, which is best for reliable street performance, offers 95+ hp @ 5500 rpm.

The Fueling/Rivera 4-valve heads accommodate almost every carburetor on the market. Special adaptors and manifolds are available upon request. For street performance, stock carburetors are fine. The dual 40mm single-throat Dell'Ortos work well for street or racing. Keep in mind, however, that dual carburetors have some tradeoffs when compared to a single carburetor. The combined force of the two-carburetor slide return springs requires that more effort be used to turn the throttle. This might or might not be a problem depending upon personal preference. The extra carburetor is good for an additional 10 horsepower, which to some negates any inconvenience (Fig. 7-18).

7-18
Here is the new three-piece manifold that utilizes two stub O-ringed intake manifolds. When properly positioned inside the plenum chamber, they allow airflow to be directed at both intake valves. This new concept (featured here with two single Dell'Ortos) is responsible for the increased flow and horsepower created by the 4-valve head design.

Using the special Rivera Stage I cam available through Rivera Engineering optimizes performance. Peak power is achieved at 5500 rpm with any Stage I combination. If a vehicle is equipped with an ignition that will allow 5500 rpm, a set of S & S semi-solid adaptors (available from Rivera Engineering) is highly recommended. Running a Stage I engine at 5000 rpm will work fine with unmodified hydraulic lifters. The Fueling/Rivera 4-valve heads are designed to accommodate cams up to .500 lift. Only those cams recommended by Rivera Engineering should be used. Using cams that are not compatible with the 4-valve heads will result in poor performance and will cause severe engine damage. Adjustable aluminum pushrods should not be used with any 4-valve combination. The combination force of two valve springs will result in pushrod deflection.

Another favorite method of increasing engine performance is by the inclusion of oversize valves, which provide added fuel intake to the combustion chamber. Though a substantial power

High-performance valves

boost is realized with performance valves, some of which allow improved flow patterns due to their design, many choose to combine new valves with supportive higher lift/longer duration cams and porting and polishing the head chamber (Fig. 7-19).

7-19
High-performance Florida Precision Calipre valves. Their new step design allows optimum airflow. Valves are marketed in stock or oversize configurations.

When oversized intake valves are used, exhaust valves are usually also modified in turn, as oversize exhaust valves will allow the engine to expel its burned gases in greater volume. When installing oversized intake valves, it is recommended that the intake ports be enlarged somewhat to correspond to the increased valve diameter. Theoretically, the prime objective of bigger valves is to increase the diametric width of the intake ports, allowing volumetrically greater amounts of vaporized fuel to enter the combustion chamber. Obtaining the proper increase in air/fuel ratio can easily be done by enlarging the ports, but it must be kept in mind that one can go overboard in the enlarging process. It is wise to use valve and sizing configurations recommended by engine experts and valve manufacturers. They have evolved sound formulas based on expertise and application.

Before undertaking an oversize valve replacement job, it is advised that proper porting specifications be obtained from a reliable Harley dealer to minimize error. If you are a bit timid about performing the modification yourself, have the dealer do it, or have it done for you by a reliable source. Dropping the new valves in after the necessary headwork is performed is a simple swap operation.

As to *what* valves to choose: Years ago you were limited, but today there are a host of offerings providing improved flow characteristics and high-strength steel alloys. Manley valves are excellent and vastly superior to Harley valves. They are of one-piece construction, stainless steel, and greatly inhibit galling. Lighter in weight than stock valves, they consequently offer greater rpm potential.

Florida Precision Caliper also markets a high-performance valve line, chosen and tried by current Harley speed record holders. These highly polished valves are shaped to enhance air/fuel flow; the portion surrounding the "tulip" or joining stem area is specially shaped, permitting more direct airflow to the cylinder, inhibiting and restricting turbulence. Since performance valves are lighter in weight than standard Harley items, they offer greater rpm potential, enabling power gains of 3 hp or better.

The associated machining procedure connected with the insertion of oversized valves is relatively simple if one has the proper tools. Necessary tools include 30-, 45-, and 60-degree circular cutters. The 30-degree stone is essential for the outer relief cut; the 45-degree stone cuts the actual valve contacting seat, and the 60-degree stone takes care of the inside relief cut (Fig. 7-20).

With care and precision, even the layman can undertake a valve reseating job with tool kits such as the one produced by Neway Manufacturing, Inc. (Fig. 7-21). These kits contain an assortment of necessary tooling that gets the job done quickly and efficiently (Fig. 7-22).

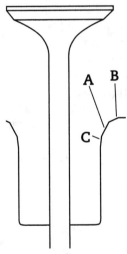

7-20
This diagram shows the three angled cuts that go into the reworking of a valve seat to accommodate oversize valves.

A - Valve seat cut
B - Top narrowing
C - Bottom narrowing

7-21
Neway sets for Harley engines include guides, cutters, handle driver, and cutter adjusting hardware.

7-22
The Neway tooling set up to cut a valve seat. The handle drives, while the angled cutter reforms the seat. Special guide rods fit into the bottom jaw of the cutter bit.

The procedure is simple. First, insert appropriate-sized pilot rod into the valve stem guide. Then place a cutter with 45-degree angle cutting blades and the same size as the valve head over the guide, and insert the cutter hex stub into the T-handle. To cut the seat angle, turn the cutter clockwise, applying just enough pressure to make the cut. Release the down pressure at the end of each cut. Center the cutting pressure end, always maintaining a downward pressure over the centerline of the pilot. Do the same for the bottom narrowing cut and the top narrowing cut, using the appropriately angled cutters.

To finish, place the valve into the seat to check for proper fit and size. Then apply lapping compound to the valve seat area and lap in the valve and seat to fine finish the seat surface. A full, explicit instruction manual is included in each Neway Kit.

Cams

You might want to augment the volumetric intake capabilities of oversized valves by adding a higher lift or extended duration cam. To obtain a foolproof compromise, study the particulars of cams produced by Sifton, Andrews, S & S, Crane, and Leinweber for varying Harley engine applications from mild to wild. Keep in mind also that longer duration cams might produce gobs of power at a higher rpm, but they are not feasible for street use. A shorter duration with a little extra lift will assist in producing smoother idle and improved throttle response when used with oversized valves. Consider the lift factor also when choosing a cam. The more lift imparted on an intake valve, the more the valve lifts out of the airflow and the more vaporized fuel charge is injected into the combustion chamber per degree of duration. On the exhaust side, the more lift realized due to the cam, the more burned exhaust gases are expelled. Unless your intake and exhaust systems can handle the added loads, either way you only stress the valvetrain with *less* return on the performance end.

Once you have studied the manuals of the leading cam manufacturers and have selected the ideal cam for your performance needs, you can alter its performance characteristics a little by advancing or retarding its rotation relative to the flywheel. As a final note, it is imperative to keep the engine running within the rev limits recommended by the cam manufacturer.

Most of the cam manufacturers listed will sell the cams separately, in kits, and also with necessary accessories such as special valve springs and retainers. A good source for cams is Rivera Engineering. They stock the cams of most manufacturers and their informative catalog lists all the characteristics pertaining to performance. It is also wise to consult with a Harley engine specialist as to what combinations work best for select situations (Fig. 7-23).

7-23
Cams of varied lifts and durations are available from Sifton, S & S, Crane, Andrews and Leinweber.

Superchargers & turbochargers

Basically power-boosting add-on units, turbochargers and superchargers (blowers) not only upgrade performance but also aesthetic value to a custom bike.

Supercharger or blower units must obtain their motivating power directly from the Harley engine, relying on either drives or belts, belts being most feasible belts. A number of mechanical blower types exist: Roots, sliding-vane, spiral, and rotary-piston. The type most applicable to Harleys is the Roots type.

Turbochargers, though not recommended for Harleys, are sometimes considered and applied; they are not as efficient as blowers. A turbocharger is a compact exhaust-driven compressor that can force more vaporized fuel into an engine than a carburetor alone can. The more air and fuel forced in, the more power gained. But turbos have their limitations, as we'll discuss, particularly in motorcycles. Turbos work more efficiently on larger car engines. When the turbo isn't pumping, smaller motorcycle engines don't have the power a car engine maintains without turbo power.

In order to properly function at the boosted cylinder pressures inaugurated, a turbo engine uses less compression (about 6:1 or 7:1), which results in sluggishness when the boost is low or the turbo is off. In motorcycle engines, turbo shortcomings such as "turbo lag" tend to be magnified. Turbo lag is the time between gas feeding and the point of acceleration kick-in. Turbos are exhaust-driven, hence they need time to achieve workable revolutions in order to compress and deliver an efficient fuel and air charge.

Most stock turbos will not operate below middle-to-high engine speeds. There is a lag period until they start up and reach efficient operating speed. Turbos can also be short-lived, since they are driven by hot exhaust gases, making the units very hot during operation. They also run at high revs during peak efficiency, which generates even more heat.

There is another inhibiting factor concerning turbocharging Harley engines: power pulse rate per engine revolution. The most powerful Harley mills deliver just two power pulses for every two crank revolutions, which aren't equally spaced. This can inhibit smooth turbo pump operation. Drawing on exhaust engine pressure for driving power tends to build up some back pressure, which can restrict the bike's exhaust system. Since this results in the engine wasting some of its horsepower to work the turbo vanes, less power is available to translate into bike driving power (Fig. 7-24).

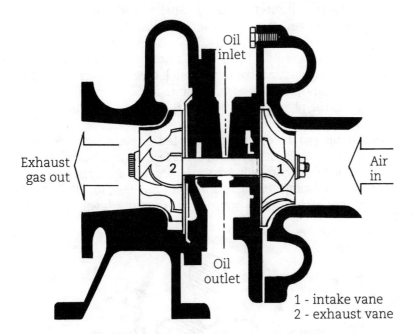

Exhaust
gas out

Oil
inlet

Air
in

Oil
outlet

1 - intake vane
2 - exhaust vane

7-24
A basic turbocharger. Exhaust gases power the turbine vane. Turbos can experience shortcomings in motorcycles. (Courtesy of American Iron. Drawing by Kelle Putman.)

Some turbochargers have been successfully applied to Harley engines. One drag-bike luminary, Harold Steele, used an early Corvair blower especially modified by Rajay to supercharge his 103-cubic inch Sportster-powered drag bike. With Steele's particular Sportster setup, the outcoming exhaust from the cylinder heads was piped to the blower through two custom-fabricated 1¾-inch diameter steel pipes, powering the exhaust-propelled side of the turbine with the waste gases expelled through a 2½-inch pipe. At the same time, by way of a common coupling, the intake turbine was actuated, turning between 80,000 and 100,000 rpm, sucking in large amounts of fuel and air through a specially machined S & S-type carburetor with a two-inch diameter throat.

Turbochargers can be applied to drag-race bikes, but are not feasible for street machines. Every once in a while, though, you will see a turbo-powered street bike, mainly in custom shows.

Superchargers lend themselves much better to Harley-Davidson engines. The most popular is the Roots-type blower, a design used on GMC Detroit Diesels. Roots blowers provide smooth, even, volumetric fuel and airflow and can generate high pressure even at slow blower speeds.

In the Roots blower, two three-lobed rotor vanes spin within the blower housing without contacting each other or their housing. The close tolerances between the rotors and housing aids in building up the high boost pressures required for efficient supercharging. Rotor rotation generates a flow rate corresponding to the engine rpm created. Supercharging by this method offers the best means to achieve optimum Harley engine power. Since the Roots blowers work most efficiently at low-range and mid-range crank speeds, they are ideal for Harley engines that also function optimally at the same levels (Fig. 7-25).

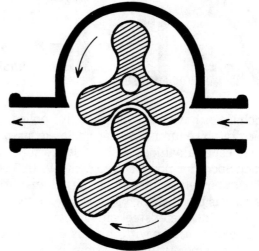

7-25
The Roots blower is the most common charger applicable to Harleys. (Courtesy of American Iron. Drawing by Kelle Putnam)

Supercharged Harley street mills should be set up using stock or lower-than-stock compression, usually about 6:1 or 7:1 for best operation. To obtain this, shave off about 0.050 inch from stock piston crowns or install properly sized replacement pistons or overbore kits. To properly set up a supercharger, consider the displacement of the blower and the displacement of the engine the blower will be mounted on. Arrive at a drive ratio that will yield no more than 10 psi (pounds per square inch) boost at the optimum crank speed the engine will be running at. Boost levels can be modified by exchanging crank and blower pulleys, which come in a variety of sizes.

Supercharging (or even turbocharging) an engine requires a lot of work, for there are virtually no aftermarket bolt-on setups available, nor any aftermarket sources for blowers exclusively designed for use on motorcycles. Years ago, the Magnuson Company (now defunct) offered a complete blower mounting kit, including a Weber DCOE carburetor, for Harley engines. They are scarce but can be hunted down, especially at swap meets. B & M has purchased all the tooling for the Magnuson superchargers, but has not to date offered a mass-produced Magnuson-type blower for motorcycle use, though they may in the future if enough demand is generated. The Magnuson 60 or 80 blowers are ideally suited for Harley-Davidson engines (Fig. 7-26).

7-26
Mark Shadley's supercharged Sportster built by Dave Perowitz. The 77.9 cubic-inch engine by Jim Thompson features the rare Magnuson blower unit and Axtell barrels.

CHAPTER 8

Brakes &
brake systems

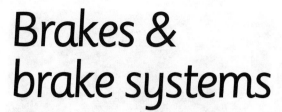

BRAKES are considered to be functional as opposed to decorative. However, due to the fact that brakes are visible on motorcycles, it is safe to assume that the better they look, the more they add to the visible impact of the custom motorcycle (Fig. 8-1).

Older, vintage bikes relied on drum brakes, but the newer Harley issues (actually from the 1960s on) all sport disk brakes. So reliable are the disks that they have become standard as stock and replacement accessory items. The catalogs abound in custom rotors, calipers, front and rear master cylinders, and the manufacturers compete heavily, trying to outdo each other in the appearance department. This has resulted in a proliferation of mild-to-wild rotor designs, some of which can do much to enhance the visual clout of a street or show bike (Figs. 8-2, 8-3).

One of the leading sources in performance braking systems is Performance Machine, Inc., of Paramount, California. They offer stock replacement or specialized systems that will outperform stock issue. Their offerings are highly stylized and of the highest quality, making their products the prime aftermarket replacement choice for all true Harley buffs. A wide assortment of rotors up to 13 inches in diameter are marketed, applicable to all Harley rear end and front end applications, which will bolt on to stock Harley wheels. Performance Machine also markets various caliper units in two-piston and four-piston versions. The two-piston units are preferable for front wheel stopping power and are less dominant on front telescopic forks or springers. The four-piston units are usually consigned to rear end stopping duties, though quite a few riders will use them up front for the added stopping power that a four-piston unit will provide.

8-1
Wyatt Fuller took a stock Harley caliper unit and grooved the faces to augment the decor of the unit.

For custom applications on vintage bikes or bikes not designed to accommodate disk brakes, the leading aftermarket brake manufacturers will provide special caliper brackets for mounting on all Harley models (Figs. 8-4 through 8-6).

8-2
This attractive stock replacement disk for Harleys is by Performance Machine. It is predrilled for lightness as well as looks.

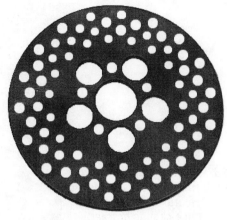

8-3
Here's another provocative stylized rotor. Units of this type are available from Performance Machine, CCI, and Drag Specialties, to name a few sources.

8-4
This bracket adapts the tiny but potent Florida Precision Caliper race-designed four-piston unit to Harley rear end applications. It can be used with stock Harley or aftermarket rotors.

8-5
Performance Machine's 137×6 caliper can be used with front stock disks and features an optional quick-change bracket.

8-6
Performance Machine's rear brake caliper, 125×4R, features four pistons, directly replaces stock unit providing optimum stopping power. It mounts in stock caliper position and utilizes stock brake lines.

Performance Machine also offers a full line of front and rear master cylinders (Fig. 8-7). The master cylinders can be obtained with activation arms or for pushrod application and can be adapted to all Harley model frames. Front handlegrip master cylinders that mount on the handlebars are also offered featuring low-profile brake fluid reservoirs. The handlegrip master cylinders are universal and the integrated powergrip levers provide maximum braking force while allowing great control sensitivity. They are available in long or short powergrip handle versions.

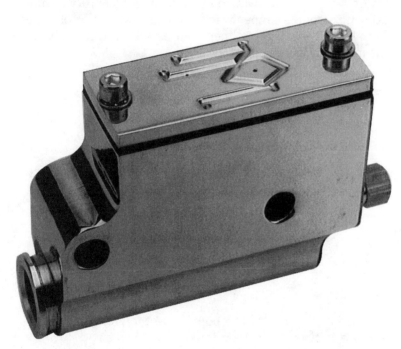

8-7
This Universal master brake cylinder for Harley precision machines is strictly for pushrod operation.

To illustrate the simplicity of a brake rotor installation or swap, we present here a typical situation. Chosen for mounting are a pair of four-piston Florida Precision Caliper brakes. This dual-caliper set-up is popular for racing machines but will apply to stock Harleys and add to the aggressive, racy appearance of the street machine. The Florida Precision Caliper units are small and compact but highly efficient and attractive (Fig. 8-8).

Disk brake installation

8-8
Florida Precision Caliper disk brake four-piston units are compact but powerful. They also feature a quick change brake pad setup—race bike-inspired but extra handy for the layman.

Figure 8-9 shows the system up on a Paughco hardtail frame, utilizing a double caliper bracket, which also can be obtained from Florida Precision Caliper. Figures 8-10 through 8-15 show the installation procedure.

8-9
The dual disk caliper setup on the special bracket; good looks plus upgraded stopping power.

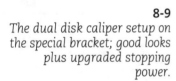

Foot controls

Forward foot controls are a popular method for foot braking and specialty controls are offered by Jay-Brake and Performance Machine. Some excellent accessory units can also be seen in the CCI and Drag Specialties catalogs.

Performance Machine offers a knockout forward control unit incorporating the master cylinder. A shift pedal assembly matching unit for the opposite side is also available and they can be purchased separately or in sets. The shift pedal matches the forward mount brake pedal and both are constructed of machined aluminum and steel. They are available for all Harley-Davidson Big Twins, 1984 and up. A special set designed for FXRs is also marketed.

8-10
The rear wheel is set into place and aligned with the axle retaining slider slots.

8-11
The axle slider and retaining nut are placed into the wheel mount slot on the thread end of the axle.

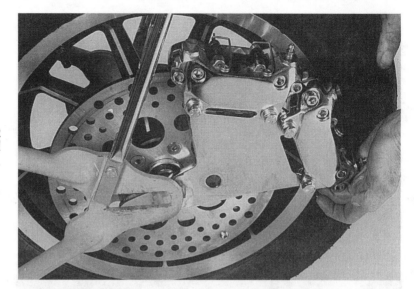

8-12
The brake setup is positioned and aligned.

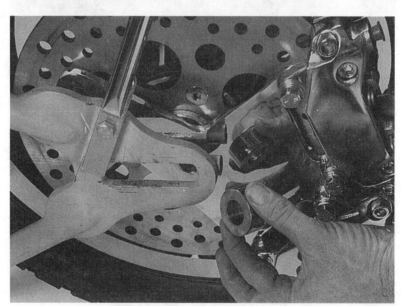

8-13
Before installing the axle in the wheel, the wheel centering spacer is placed on the brake side of the frame.

The brake pedal is mounted forward of the foot peg in order to provide immediate braking response without having to lift the foot from the peg. Brake pedal position is fully adjustable through the implementation of a splined shaft, the return stop

8-14
The axle is fed through the frame and wheel bearings and secured by the retaining nut on the rear rigid frame tab on the other side of the frame.

8-15
The caliper plate tab is then secured to the inside frame leg with a bolt threading into the frame. This anchors the plate and prevents it from spinning on the axle when the bike is moving.

internal for a clean appearance. Both assemblies are bolt-on replacement units; shift pedal assemblies for late model FXRs include shift rod and backing plate (Figs. 8-16, 8-17).

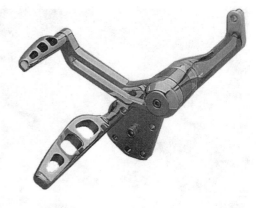

8-16
Performance Machine master cylinder and foot peg assembly for '84 to present Harley-Davidson Big Twins.

8-17
Performance Machine shift pedal assembly coordinates in styling with the master cylinder-foot peg unit.

Brake lines

Brake lines must receive consideration also. Most stock issue lines are unsightly, encouraging the use of more visually efficient approaches that enhance rather than detract from the overall looks of the bike. The hot setup today is braided brake lines, such as those offered by Russell and Spectre (Fig. 8-18). Spectre offers full braided lines or braided sheathing that can be applied over existing brake lines (Fig. 8-19). Of these alternatives, the braided lines are preferred, though a bit more costly. They are easy to install with specially designed torque fittings that make brake line installation a snap (Figs. 8-20 through 8-23).

Regardless of whether you opt for looks or stopping power, you can see that you have an optional array of brake system aftermarket alternatives that will add an extra touch of class to your personalized vehicle.

8-18
Braided lines are good-looking and offer major protection for brake fluid hoses.

8-19
Spectre braided tubing can be slaved over existing stock lines. Spectre also offers pre-braided hose in special packages.

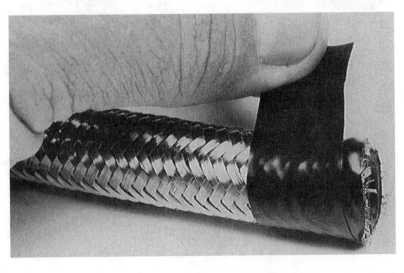

8-20
To prepare the Spectre hose to accept the torque fittings, the ends must first be wrapped with Spectre flex-tape.

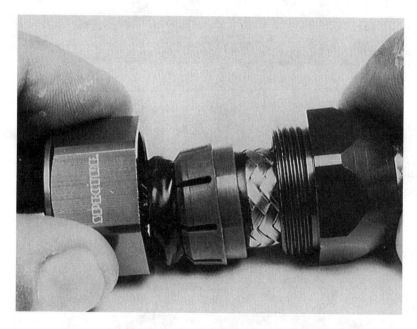

8-21
The sealing ferrule is placed over the taped end as shown.

8-22
The torque fitting ends are then placed over the hose and ferrule.

8-23
Tighten the connection with a wrench and the result is a solid, attractive connection. Spectre torque-fittings come in a host of anodized colors.

Ornamentation

ORNAMENTATION can add a finishing touch to any motorcycle, whether fully customized or basic. It also provides an avenue for self-expression by individualizing the bike to the owner's taste. A wide array of bike ornaments are available to the customizer. Ornamentation can be home-brewed, or customized from "store-bought" accessories, or simply added as individual components. The bulk of ornamental add-ons are available through Harley-Davidson or aftermarket motorcycle accessory shops. Art supply and craft stores can provide some of the necessary sundries, while a wealth of ornamental refinement parts may be obtained by mail order, shopping through Custom Chrome, Inc.; Drag Specialties; and Paughco, Inc. catalogs. The degree of ornamentation depends upon individual taste, ingenuity, and budget.

In this chapter we will cover add-on ornamentation as well as the modification of existing components. We can only scratch the surface here, but the ideas shown might inspire you to make your own statement in the customizing process.

Nuts & fasteners

Simple fastening hardware can add a decorative touch when you use custom Colony nuts, available from such sources as Custom Chrome, Inc. (CCI) and Drag Specialties.

Colony nuts come in various types (acorn, spike, cap, and the new "krommets," also known as bullets) that can effectively serve to dress up chrome dresser panels and mounted accessories (Fig. 9-1). Cross-reference lists are offered in the accessory catalogs to help you select the proper Harley decorative hardware.

Grips

Handgrips are basic, and all Harley owners are familiar with the stock grips that are offered with stock bikes. These can, however, be fashionably decorated so that even *they* can work in with the decorative motif of the motorcycle, or be dressed up to gain attention.

9-1
Here, a rear-brake caliper unit and swing arm are gracefully ornamented with chromed Colony acorn nuts. Nut swaps are simple, but evoke that added decorative touch.

Many bikers will strip off the rubber grip coatings and replace them with custom-made leather handlegrips or grip covers. This usually entails the removal of the cushions, then taking the grip unit to a leather specialist who can recover them to the owner's taste (Fig. 9-2).

Accessory grips are also offered by aftermarket shops and accessory mail outlets, and are much more decorative than the more mundane stock grips. Drag Specialties and CCI both offer sets with inlaid Harley-Davidson emblems and shields on the chromed ends.

The newest idea on the market is the Soft Touch Blue Dot grip offered by CCI. The Blue Dot grips offer the same neoprene grip coverings as typical standard units, but include blue lens end-cap centers with a 1½ watt bulb to light up the blue dot. The special internal bulb and socket are designed to absorb the common handlebar vibrations inherent with most V-twins. The Blue Dots will mount on all Harley models from 1973 on up.

9-2
Linda Ferraro had her grips custom-covered in leather, hand-stitched to match the color inserts on her seat. Grips are CCI's Blue Dot grips, which contain blue dot ends that actually light up for a novel touch.

Plate brackets

License plates do not add much to the aesthetics of a bike, but can take on a decorative dimension when housed in one of the many custom license plate frames marketed by various accessory companies. Many of these are chromed frames with H-D designations and emblems, while others are more ornate. CCI features billet aluminum frames and louvered license backing plates as well as anodized and engraved frames in red, blue, and black. Drag Specialties offers eagle license frames in chrome and gold, as well as a special Night-Lighter frame featuring an array of six red lights that flash in sequence and appear to rotate around the plate frame. The Night-Lighter is available with red lights and a red lens, or multi-colored lights and a smoke lens. Special knock-outs allow fitting to any motorcycle license plate. Check with your local aftermarket accessory dealers and you will discover that they carry an extensive line of decorative brackets (Fig. 9-3).

Emblems

Emblems are easily integrated into bikes and bike components, and a vast array are marketed by the major accessory manufacturers such as CCI and Drag Specialties. They are also carried by Harley-Davidson dealers and aftermarket accessory shops (Fig. 9-4). Emblems are used lavishly and sometimes wantonly on H-D motorcycles, helmets, boots, saddlebags, and just about anywhere else they will mount. They are also popular for adding to clothing. One favorite place to mount large eagles or H-D shield emblems is on the rear of sissy rails. A number of Harley-issue rails are easily adapted for mounting a host of available H-D emblems.

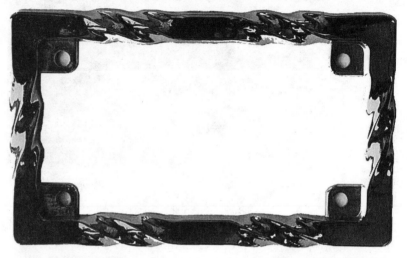

9-3
This twisted chrome bracket is sturdy as well as attractive. Units are marketed in chrome and gold.

9-4
Examples of emblems by CCI. At the top and bottom are the V-twin eagle emblems; in the middle is the US legend emblem.

Dash panels

The noticeable gap between the dual Harley fat-bob tanks leaves much to be desired and should be concealed. Stock, decorative, and custom-fabricated panels can be used to enhance the tank configuration (Figs. 9-5 through 9-7). We can study some custom-tailored dash panels decorated in full leather with conchos and other inlaid material.

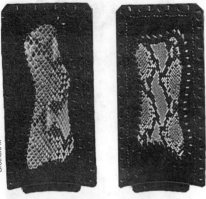

9-5
Snakeskin panels by Durty Bill. Fine leathercrafting and the insertion of snakeskin panels make these units stand out.

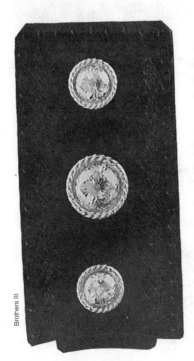

9-6
Here are two more Durty Bill panels sporting different ornate conchos. Intaglio borderwork and inlaid embossing also individualize these pieces.

These are the handiwork
of Durty Bill, considered
one of the most creative
leathercraft wizards in
the country. Durty will
also match seats and
other relative
ornamentation to follow
through a dash panel
design motif such as this
one.

Panels can also be made
to order. Many materials
can tie into the
fabrication of dash
panels, and a host of
original pieces can be
found in most accessory
retail shops (Fig. 9-8).
Similar custom dash
panels contoured in
leather and Naugahyde
can also be obtained from
CCI, though these are not
as ornate. CCI offers dash
panels for XFR, FXST, and
FLST model Harleys.

9-7
*This Durty Bill piece sports an
eagle medallion concho and dual-
inlay lace-edged panels.*

Auto ornaments

At times, automotive ornamentation can be implemented to
customize or decorate a bike or component part. Figure 9-9
shows a novel use for a car hood ornament that Ron Finch used
to grace a chopped, small, front custom fender to create a
decorative effect. Finch first fashioned a baseplate to add some
dimension and style to the basic ornament. The ornamental
assembly was then secured to the stubby Finch fender with two
bolts, which went from the underside of the fender, through
the baseplate, and into two original mounting holes situated in
the ornament structure.

9-8
A Finch fat-bob custom featuring a unique custom-contoured leather panel section. Edge lacing, embossed initials and leather-laced conchos add a finishing touch.

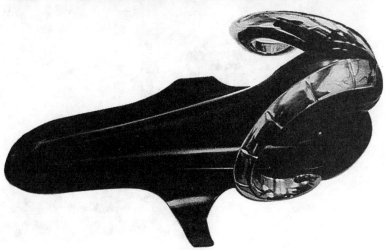

9-9
This hood ornament is mounted on a chopped front fender. The decorative fender is unique and eye-catching— definitely distinctive. The ornament is affixed underneath by means of two bolts, which screw into the baseplate and ornament.

Ornamentation 217

Conchos

You are probably familiar with the conchos that are used to decorate clothing and apparel. There are also unlimited decorative applications for conchos on motorcycles (Fig. 9-10). Conchos can be readily obtained at leathercraft and art supply stores and are offered in a multitude of styles and sizes (Fig. 9-11).

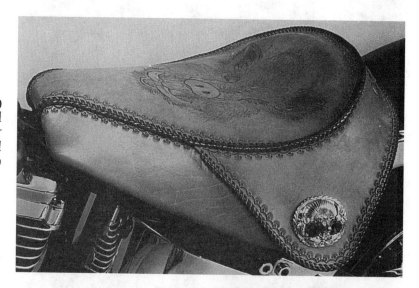

9-10
Dave Lumsden coordinated two conchos into the decor of this custom-tailored motorcycle seat. Many concho styles are marketed.

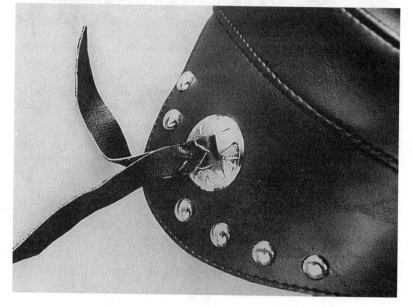

9-11
Tie-on conchos offer another style, here used as a decorative medium on a seat.

There are unlimited possibilities for the application of conchos as bike ornaments. They can be used to trim or accent saddlebags, seats, gusseted areas, gas caps, carburetor and side covers, and even fenders.

Here is a unique application of screw-fastened conchos on a front fender that I fashioned. (Fig. 9-12). These ornate engraved conchos in silver come in a variety of sizes and can be mixed or matched—whatever suits your fancy. Different sizes were selected to work as a sort of fender rib pattern with the conchos progressing in size from the middle to the narrower end sections.

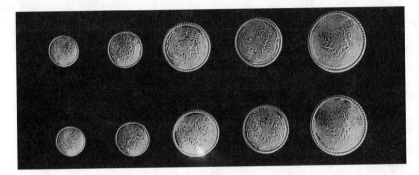

9-12
One style of engraved, embossed conchos can be screw-mounted from the rear, which makes them ideal for mounting on steel, leather, or any material not exceeding ⅛ inch in thickness. This style was chosen for decorating the fiberglass fender illustrated in the next six photos.

The technique for applying conchos is as follows: First, it is helpful to find the centerline for positioning the centrally located conchos. This is done by measuring across the fender at various points along the circumference of the fender from edge to edge (Fig. 9-13). After you have found the centerline, run a tape along this line to indicate the central points over the length of the fender. Then mark off the centerline of the fender from the front to the back end. This is so you can properly position the conchos to fit along the fender length at equal start and finish points from each end of the fender.

From the centerline, measure off location distances for the conchos. You can place the conchos in position and trace them onto the fender to give you an idea of the pattern that is evolving. In this example, the fender was measured and drilled prior to painting, which I highly recommend. After painting, you run the risk of scratching or misdrilling, which are hard to

Ornamentation 219

9-13
Measuring across the fender from edge to edge will give you the centerline. Do this every 6 inches along the fender. At this point, the edge-to-edge distance was 9 inches, so the centerline was at 4½ inches.

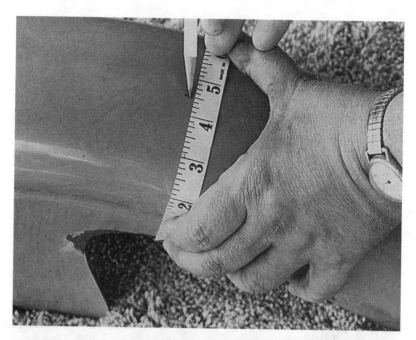

9-14
Concho centerpoint locations. If done correctly, the conchos will be properly positioned. This procedure should simplify concho placement.

9-15
Screw-on conchos mount simply by means of a flat screwdriver, which secures from the underside of the fender. In the case of fiberglass fenders, do not tighten down as tightly as you would on a steel fender, as you can crack or damage the mounting area.

correct on a painted unit. Besides, it's easier to pencil measurements onto primed stock. After concho locations have been determined, you can mark off the central drilling location points by cutting out the centers along the tape (Fig. 9-14).

The next step involves drilling the concho fastening-screw holes, which should be drilled out with a battery-powered hand drill or electric screwdriver. A regular drill bit was used to drill out the fiberglass fender. Carbide steel bits are recommended for steel fenders.

The final step, mounting the conchos, is the easiest part of the procedure. The concho screw fasteners are placed into the holes, and the conchos are started by rotating them onto the threads protruding on the fender top. Then tighten down the underside screws with a flathead screwdriver (Fig. 9-15). When you're finished, you'll have a well-decorated, novel fender to admire (Fig. 9-16).

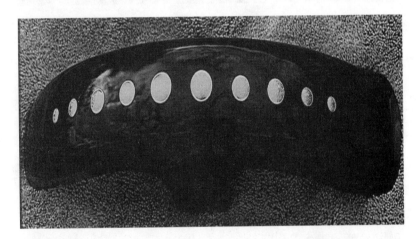

9-16
The complete conch-embellished fender. The fender is custom-designed by Frenchies Fiberglass Novelties, Pompano Beach, Fla.

Engraving

Engraving is the old silversmith's art, but it's still popular and very attractive when applied to chrome, aluminum, gold, and anodized metal surfaces. Most people who do engraving are specialists and in most cases not bikers, though some scattered bike shops do deal in engraving. For the most part, engraving is sent out to the specialists who ply their trade in the jewelry, gun, and silver businesses.

9-17
This decorative point cover is available from Sumax, a custom parts specialst.

Engraving on custom and street vehicles is attaining much popularity as a form of ornamentation. For the more conservative-minded, companies such as CCI offer a host of engraved parts that can be purchased at Harley accessory dealerships or mail-ordered from the CCI catalog. These parts include sprocket, pulley, point covers, etc., in anodized aluminum; these really stand out when mounted (Figs. 9-19 through 9-21). Also available from sources such as Harley-Davidson, Drag Specialties, and

9-18
Another engraved item by Sumax is this pulley cover insert. Similar pieces are available as stock items from Drag Specialties and CCI.

CCI are engraved mirrors, which add an extra ornamental touch to the bike.

Show custom builders and riders usually rely on self-styled design engraving to embellish their parts to fortify the overall aesthetics of the bike. Since specialty engraving shops are few and far between, most cognizant custom builders avail themselves of the services of Sumax, a custom parts and accessory source that also specializes in motorcycle component engraving. Sumax's own engraver, Herb Jerred (Fig. 9-20), is the leader with a classic, accepted technique second to none in motorcycle decor circles. Herb utilizes a method of cutting, then highlighting the cuts with stippling. Stippling acts as a shading and comprises a multitude of carefully executed dots (Figs. 9-21 through 9-23). The Sumax catalog lists all of their engraving services and standard parts that come pre-engraved. Specialized engraving must be discussed with Sumax, which will provide price quotes on desired designwork.

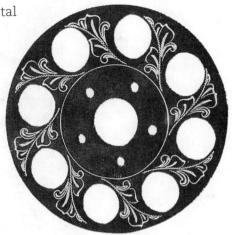

9-19
Here's yet another Sumax design on a pulley insert. Pulley inserts are powder-coated in any color choice desired on a special-order basis.

9-20
Herb Jerred at work on a Harley part. Jerred is the leading motorcycle parts engraver in the country.

Ornamentation 223

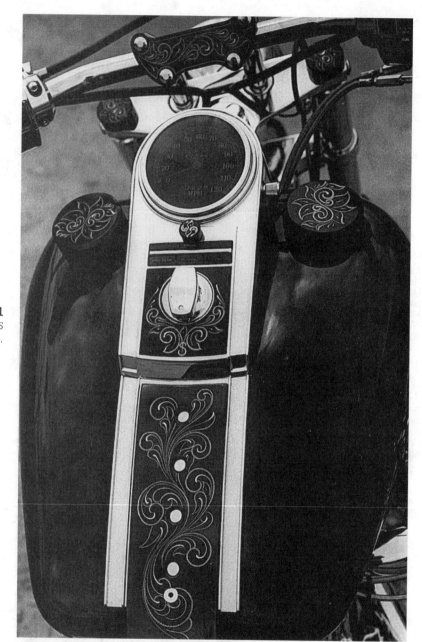

9-21
Here are some other examples of Jarred's classic handiwork.

9-22
Here's an engraved motif
applied to an engine case.

9-23
Notice how the tastefully
integrated etching adds a
touch of class to the frame,
pulley, and cover components.

Ornamentation allows each Harley owner the license to individualize a bike so that it will be distinctive and more attractive. There is no end to what can be done—depending, of course, on individual ingenuity, taste, and pocketbook (Figs. 9-24, 9-25).

9-24
Engraving and etching can also be carried into mirrors. Accessory engraved mirrors are marketed by Harley-Davidson, CCI, and Drag Specialties.

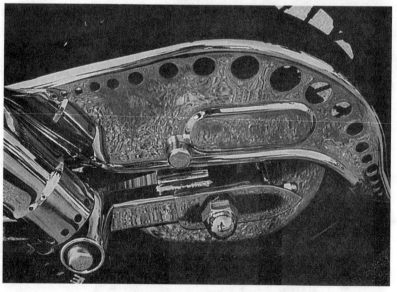

9-25
Here is another example of tasteful ornamentation. Prior to chroming, this chain cover was drilled out in a progressive pattern.

Super-modified customs

IN THE PRECEDING chapters you have seen what is available, and some approaches you can take in modifying your stock Harley-Davidson. This chapter focuses on the end product: classic customs that incorporate some of these customizing techniques, and that personify their owners' individual tastes (Fig. 10-1). The line of demarcation between a motorcycle as a vehicle and a motorcycle as an art object narrows as more and more enthusiasts choose to go the radical route in customizing their bikes.

10-1
Ron Finch's Aorta is a 1975 Shovelhead-powered machine with Dell'Orto carburetor, VL springer, and no conventional gas-tank setup. The gas tank is in the enclosed rear fender, which holds four gallons. Fuel is fed to the motor via an electric fuel pump.

One of the most radical bike builders, and also one of the most highly creative and artistic, is Ron Finch, who helped elevate the motorcycle to the state of kinetic art that it maintains today in custom shows and circles. His shop, Finch's Custom Styled Cycles, is located in Pontiac, Michigan. Countless bikes have rolled out of that shop to win hundreds of trophies for Finch. Consequently, Finch motorcycles are highly sought-after to appear in custom shows.

Ron Finch is considered the Renaissance man of motorcycle customizers, and may well be the first custom bike designer to have his work shown in art museums. He was the first to present bikes in the 58th Michigan's Artist exhibit at the all-state biennial for painters and sculptors.

Finch is an ingenious designer and an excellent painter—one of the best. His metalwork and sculpture are both unique and flawless. His creative approach is fresh and different—highly stylized but aesthetically correct and innovative. Following are a few examples of his creations from mild to wild.

Odin's Axle

Odin's Axle is Finch's tour-de-force custom, featured in *Motorcycle World* as the best U.S. custom. It is a bike that's way ahead of its time (Fig. 10-2).

One of the high points of *Odin's Axle* is the paint job, which encompasses every color of the spectrum, though the basic overall colors are in varied shades of blue. Finch estimates that the paint alone for *Axle* cost $1,100 and took five weeks to apply, even with an assistant's help. The cool blue underbase is topped with sky-blue metalflake on the left side. Also found on the left side is a dynamic, eye-catching 14-karat gold-leaf freak panel on the neck. This panel is composed of hand brushwork.

The right side of the bike sports paintwork in blue Murano pearl. A metal, pretzelwork relief design adorns the tank, in hues going from one side of the color wheel to the other. The top of the tank is highlighted with a combination of pearlescent and flake, then decorated with interwoven multi-colored scallops (Figs. 10-3, 10-4).

10-2
Odin's Axle is a Finch pièce de résistance. *The bike took almost a year in construction time between other scheduled jobs. It is almost entirely hand-constructed and is modified throughout.*

10-3
This large tank is custom-designed and features intricate sheetmetal work and molding throughout. Note the novel effect achieved with the zig-zag rodwork motif on the side of the tank. The Panhead engine uses SU carburetion.

10-4
Side view of the neck area profiles the unique lines of this highly stylized custom. Note the extensive modification to the springer, particularly in the neck area. Though asymmetric, the springer is fully functional.

The wildest structure on the bike is the front end. Really "out of sight," this chromed front end, originally an early BSA springer, is a classic example of asymmetric design. The legs were extended 38 inches. The left side is composed of three hatchets. The right fork leg is completely different, utilizing a pretzeling effect in steel rod, fully chromed. A 21-inch wheel rim laced to a Husqvarna hub completes the front-end package (Fig. 10-5).

The hatchet motif follows through on the rear end in the hardtail frame, and in the taillights, which are fashioned of two handmade axes, with lenses also fabricated by hand. The rear wheel rim is an 18-inch Triumph type laced to a Harley hub. Small scratchbuilt hatchets cover the circumference of the rear as well as the front hub.

Ace's Toy

A representative example of a hot street machine is Ace Armstrong's 1991 Sturgis converted along cafe racer lines, conceived by Ace and built at Peterson's Harley-Davidson shop in North Miami, Florida (Fig. 10-6).

10-5
A close-up view of the asymmetric springer detailing. Lots of hours went into its fabrication, transforming it into a work of sculptured steel art.

10-6
*Ace Armstrong's Toy is a street beater with Ness design
influence, a "show" as well as "go" piece built at Peterson's
Harley-Davidson, where Ace serves as manager.*

Originating as a Dyna-Glide, the machine underwent a
cosmetic facelift as well as a complete engine overhaul to
tweak it out and give it more street bite. The major boost in
horsepower came with the addition of the Fueling-Rivera 4-
valve heads and the Screamin' Eagle carb setup and ignition
package. To provide ominous stopping power, a custom dual
disc brake setup was added; the rear wheel is a solid disc
Harley wheel with decorative milling work by Wyatt Fuller.

Body cosmetics include a Ness race fairing, lower down-tube air
dam, a trick orange, white, black paint job, and an originally
styled airbrushed bar and shield Harley emblem. The trim seat
is the slim-styled Corbin "Gunfighter" unit (Fig. 10-7).

232 Customizing Your Harley

10-7
The powerful engine realizes its muscle from the Fueling-Rivera 4-valve head setup and Harley "Screamin' Eagle" carb and ignition. Extensive chrome by Atlantic Coast Plating gives the engine components their jewel-like aura.

After 16 years in the custom bike business, Dave Perowitz of Brockton, Massachusetts, has earned a reputation as one of the finest bike builders around. His bikes have graced the covers and pages of such magazines as *Easyriders* and *Hot Bike*. His work is unique and flawless, creative and distinctive. He excels as a painter and graphics designer and his styling is always in keeping with the times.

One great Perowitz machine is Stan White's fairing-equipped Evolution Low Rider street screamer (Fig. 10-8). The bike features—in addition to a Perowitz paint job—a collective two-into-one Ness exhaust system, Rev-Tech front wheel, Performance Machine brakes, and a specially designed custom seat by Danny Grey. The engine sports an add-on 1989 Harley Screamin' Eagle kit, with the engine refined by Jim Thompson. (See Appendix for supplier addresses.)

Dave Perowitz cycle fabrications

10-8
Stan White's Evolution-powered Perowitz creation is decked out with a fairing and features a Ness exhaust system with collective two-into-one exhaust pipes.

10-9
Attention to detail, tasteful powder coating, and coordinated paint make Pristine, a late Evolution Big Twin cradled in a hardtail custom frame, an eye-catching showpiece.

Built as a project by Sumax owner Kirk Van Scoten, *Pristine* is a billboard for the quality products, services, and styling concepts provided by this avant-garde distributor. The bike features a late-model Big Twin Evolution motor in a Sumax hardtail frame and is loaded with powder-coating and a host of Sumax goodies: Jay brake forward controls, Sumax rotors, Jay brake calipers, and Russell braided lines (Figs. 10-9, 10-10).

10-10
Pristine's left side is as clean and detailed as the right. A wide glide front end was chosen, custom detailed in powder coating and chrome.

The paint job is a graphically simple but eye-catching study in black and white. A special feature is the sleek custom oil tank, which comes with the custom rigid frame. The engine is a stock 80 with a Rivera Spirit cam added, SU carb, adjustable pushrods, and some mild flow work on the heads; air cleaner is a production Sumax item with coordinating graphics (Fig. 10-11).

In the early to mid-1970s, the "cafe racer" began to evolve, pioneered by such notables as Arlen Ness, owner of Arlen Ness Enterprises, San Leandro, California. Ness was reknowned for building customs and street bikes for speed when he began designing and marketing components geared toward performance. Cafe racers are popular to this day, but do not

Arlen Ness's cafe racer

10-11
Close-up detailing of tank and engine. Barrels and heads are powder-coated as well as the engine cases with liberal touches of chrome throughout.

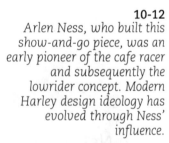

10-12
Arlen Ness, who built this show-and-go piece, was an early pioneer of the cafe racer and subsequently the lowrider concept. Modern Harley design ideology has evolved through Ness' influence.

share the impact or popularity of the lowrider, which is more conducive to long-range street riding and hence is favored by street custom buffs.

Ness's cafe racer was built around a late Evolution engine and was a feature attraction at Daytona in 1990, where it was raffled off (Figs. 10-12, 10-13). The bike features a host of Ness-

10-13
Closeup of the motor and underseat styling panel on Ness collector exhaust—trick and neat.

designed aftermarket parts, which are produced in flawless fiberglass. Ness also manufactures custom seats and is acknowledged as the master of motorcycle engine supercharging. Fenders, seat, fairing, and fiberglass components are marketed by Arlen Ness Enterprises, and are known for their quality and durability as well as their easy-mount capability (Fig. 10-14).

10-14
The Ness styled fairing is compact and aesthetically and aerodynamically sound; it's exactingly designed for ease of installation.

Arlen Ness can be credited with the innovation of many of the styling concepts seen today, particularly in "lowrider" circles.

Turbo-cruiser

Custom Accessories of Pompano Beach, Florida, aside from being a quality parts shop, is well-known in the area for building righteous speed, custom, and street bikes. Steve Jackobowski, builder Jim Camene, and engine specialist Scott Baringer were responsible for this outrageous turbocharged, fuel-injected 1984 FXST with a modified 1990 Evolution Big Twin motor (Fig. 10-15). With trimmed pistons and heads, the tweaked motor features an I.H.I. turbo unit with a home-brewed fuel injection system devised by Baringer. The show-piece sports lots of chrome enhancement as well as a host of anodized goodies. Most appealing to onlookers, the machine

10-15
Designed and built at Custom Accessories of Pompano, this Harley FXST features a turbo and fuel injection.

has taken many trophies in the radical street machine class in local shows. The magnificent paint job is by Chris Cruz (Figs. 10-16, 10-17).

Owner Sandy Roca of Wellesley Hills, Massachusetts—reknowned motorcycle expert, photographer, and prolific contributor to major custom motorcycle magazines for the past 25 years—can qualify as a major custom innovator, even though he only works on his own personal machines (Fig. 10-18). His unique street chopper was built around a 1973 Shovelhead. Cradled in a single loop frame molded by Dave Perowitz (who also did the monochromatic paint job), the project took Roca four years to finish; it was built from the ground up. The frame was built by Bill Gruhlke of Santa Cruz and incorporates a 40-degree neck rake, with trees raked an additional degree. The downtube was also stretched three inches.

Prize privateer

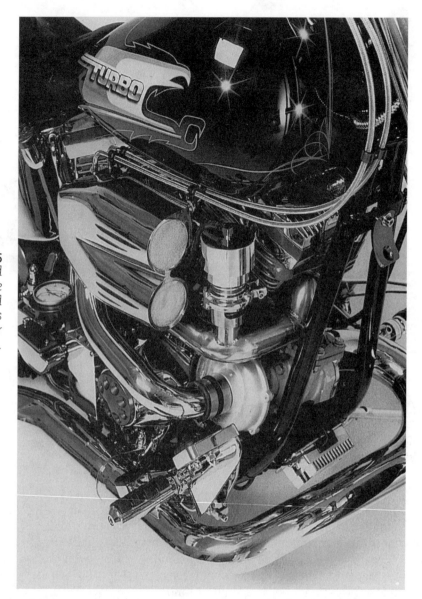

10-16
Closeup of the detailed engine, showing the turbocharger mounted behind the front chassis down tubes and the fuel injecting pumper system.

10-17
The electronic "brain box" for the fuel injection setup shown with the cover off. Baringer supervised the electronic work on the machine.

10-18
The long, lean lines of Roca's privateer custom give it an aggressive look that's typically "chopper."

Other dominant features that catch the eye include: clear primary cover of high-impact plastic, rear Wassel aluminum fender, solo sprung seat, tubular rear fender strut, Drag Specialties air cleaner, Mandrel bent stainless steel pipes, Morris mags, Rickman glide front forks, Honda disc front brakes, and a Vincent Black Shadow rear (drum) brake (Figs. 10-19, 10-20).

10-19
Engine work is immaculate; cases are bead-blasted for a satin finish, with touches of chrome here and there.

Hog High

Hog High, a unique street machine owned and built by Dave Lumsden of Hog High Cycle Works, Ft. Lauderdale, Florida, is unique in the truest sense of the word and a consistent show winner everywhere it is exhibited. *Hog High* took first place in the Ft. Lauderdale autorama show, first in the West Coast Easyriders custom show, and first in the 1990 Daytona Rats Hole show, beating all class opposition (Fig. 10-21). Its uniqueness lies in the fact that the entire bike frame, tanks, and fenders are not painted, but flawlessly black-chrome plated. The only artistic embellishment is the artwork added to the tanks and derby cover by airbrush wizard Dawn of Air-Craft, Ft. Lauderdale, Florida.

The bike is a 1984 FXST with chrome plating done by Al at Atlantic Coast Plating (Fig. 10-22). For roadability, Lumsden relies on a fully stock Evolution suspension system with stock rake, no fork extension to the Wide Glide telescopic forks. Footboards were chosen instead of standard footpegs for added rider comfort. The oil tank, risers, and front fender are stock issue. A Heritage fender was chosen for the rear.

10-21
Hog High is a flawless lowrider with frame, tanks, and fenders black chrome plated. All plating on the machine was by Atlantic Coast Plating, Ft. Lauderdale, Florida.

Twisted Sisters

Hailing from Lauderhill, Florida, Jeff Dilworth first purchased his bike for the relatively modest sum of $5,000. After a complete facelift, the bike now carries a value of $25,000 and has won a host of trophies in local custom shows.

The highlight of this magnificent hog is the modified Harley stock frame. The frame is the superlative handiwork of Larry Scheffauer, who dedicated three months of time to the radical sculpturing project. The frame was secured in a frame machine, and each twisted area was cut and twisted a section at a time with refined torch and construction work. Assembly and fusion welding were done using tungsten steel. Extensive grinding work was added to fine finish the frame (Fig. 10-23).

10-22
Mural work is by Dawn of Air-Craft. The bike has taken top trophies in major custom shows throughout the country.

10-23
Twisted Sisters, a '60s-styled chopper, features a hand-made twisted steel frame, twisted steel high sissy bar, and long, lean styling.

Twisted Sisters' tank is also custom-modified. The stock bottom plate of a Sportster tank was cut out, as well as the tunnel channel. A flat plate was welded in place under the tank and chromed on the underside. The tank mounts high on the frame and adds to the overall chopper profile (Fig. 10-24).

The front end was structurally built by a dude known in bikedom as J.W., who hangs his helmet in Pittsburgh, Pennsylvania. J.W. also fabricated the sissy rail and homebrewed handlebars specifically for the bike.

The bike was completed by Heaven on Wheels, Oakland Park, Florida. The special paintwork was laid on by the author, who was also responsible for the muralwork.

American Excess

Bankrolled and owned by John Morton, *American Excess* is the end result of a no-holds-barred, lavish revamping of a 1988 FXRS. Morton put his head together with fellow biker Serge Avsenew and came up with the outrageous, opulent features that make the machine stand out on the street or showroom

10-24
High-mount Sportster tank, radical neck rake reflects '60s chopper look. Note the first-class molding and twisted down tubes.

floor. Morton found the mint FXRS at a local Harley-Davidson dealer, then went over it for the full-tilt facelift, which included engine and tranny work, brakes, chrome plating, an abundance of gold plating on bolts and parts, and a paint job so clear it looks as if you could swim in it (Figs. 10-25, 10-26).

10-25
Lots of gold and chrome and an opulent paint job make American Excess a classic showpiece.

10-26
Left side is also immaculately detailed. Machine is valued at over $30,000.

The Indy green base coat was laid over Black Pearl by Bob Thorne, who also molded in the frame to the utmost degree. The *tour de force* is the detailed, modified facsimile of the American Express charge card rendered onto the sides of the tanks by superb muralist Dawn of Air-Craft, in Ft. Lauderdale, Florida. The motorcycle's year and serial number were used as the card number in exacting detail, right down to the raised three-dimensional lettering as found on actual American Express cards.

All the mechanical and construction work on the bike was done by Jerry Turner.

Felix Lugo's *Intimidation*, styled along the Bay Area lowrider theme, is probably the lowest of lowriders, with the frame sitting as low as 2½ inches off the ground. Lugo, an architect, was greatly influenced by Arlen Ness and styled *Intimidation* with Ness's concepts in mind (Figs. 10-27, 10-28).

Intimidation

10-27
Intimidation, *a popular show-and-go piece, was featured in two major magazines,* American Iron *and* Hot Bike. *Bike features nitrous oxide boost and the nitrous bottle can be seen mounted on the hardtail rear.*

10-28
Intimidation boasts an extremely low profile.

The bike took Lugo two years to build from the time he acquired it as a 1972 XLH. On completion, the bike was featured in *American Iron* magazine. The frame is a modified Santee hardtail and the bulk of the custom refurbishing was undertaken at Bill's Bikes in West Palm Beach, Florida. Special features of the bike include a nitrous oxide injection system by Nitrous Oxide Systems, Cypress, California, and a blue pearl paint overcoat by Tanners Customs. Mural work was by Lucia Syzmanik.

Suppliers

Gary Bang, Inc.
Box 472
Canoga Park, CA 91305

Chrome Specialties
3227 W. Euless Blvd.
Euless, TX 76040

Custom Chrome, Inc. (CCI)
1 Jacqueline Court
Morgan Hill, CA 95037

Cycle Fabrications
909 N. Main St.
Brockton, MA 02401

Drag Specialties
9839 W. 69th St.
Eden Prairie, MN 55344

Eagle Iron Parts & Accessories
3700 W. Juneau Ave.
Milwaukee, WI 53201

Harley-Davidson
Genuine Accessories
3700 W. Juneau Ave.
Milwaukee, WI 53201

Heaven on Wheels Custom
Cycles and Accessories
1052 E. Oakland Park Blvd.
Oakland Park, FL 33334

Jammer Cycle Products
6417 San Fernando Rd.
Glendale, CA 91201

Mustang Motorcycle Products
Box 29
Terryville, CT 06786

Arlen Ness Enterprises
15997 E. 14th St.
San Leandro, CA 94578

Sumax Cycle Products
337 Clear Rd.
Oriskany, NY 13424

Accessory parts

Jaybrake Enterprises, Inc.
211 Grant St.
Lockport, NY 14094

Performance Machine, Inc.
15220 Illinois Ave.
Paramount, CA 90723

Rivera Engineering
6416 S. Western Ave.
Whittier, CA 90606

Brakes

Carburetors & manifolds

Custom Chrome, Inc.
1 Jacqueline Court
Morgan Hill, CA 95037

Drag Specialties
9839 W. 69th St.
Eden Prairie, MN 55344

Keihin Seiki U.S.A.
7271 Garden Grove Blvd.
Garden Grove, CA 92641

Mikuni American Corp.
8910 Mikuni Ave.
Northridge, CA 91324

Ram Jett
Box 1521
Santa Maria, CA 93456

Rivera Engineering
6416 S. Western Ave.
Whittier, CA 90606

S&S Performance Carburetors
Box 215
Viola, WI 54664

Finishing

Kosmoski's House of Kolor
2521 27th Ave. S.
Minneapolis, MN 55406

Metalflake Corp.
Amesbury, MA 01913

Ditzler-PPG
Box 3510
Troy, MI 48084

Frames

Paughco, Inc.
11 Cowee Dr.
Carson City, NV 89701

Santee Industries
651 Arroyo St.
San Fernando, CA 90606

Sumax Cycle Products
337 Clear Rd.
Oriskany, NY 13424

Front ends

Paughco, Inc.
11 Cowee Dr.
Carson City, NY 89701
• *Springers*

Forking by Frank
945 Pitner
Evanston, IL 60202
• *Extended fork tubes*

Accel
175 N. Branford Rd.
Branford, CT 06045

Morris Magnetos, Inc.
103 Washington St.
Morristown, NJ 07960

Ignition

Hunt Magneto
11336-A Sunco Dr.
Rancho Cordova, CA 95742

Screamin Eagle
Performance Products
3700 W. Juneau Ave.
Milwaukee, WI 53201

Crane Cams
530 Fentriss Blvd.
Daytona Beach, FL 32014

Rivera Engineering
6416 S. Western Ave.
Whittier, CA 90606

Performance cams

Leinbweber Enterprises
17579 Mesa Rd.
Hesperia, CA 92345

Sifton Motorcycle Products
943 Branston Rd.
San Carlos, CA 94070

Sumax
337 Clear Rd.
Oriskany, NY 13424

Powder coating

Corbin Saddle
123-C Lee Rd.
Watsonville, CA 95077

Drag Specialties
9839 W. 69th St.
Eden Prairie, MN 55344

Seats

Custom Chrome, Inc.
1 Jacqueline Court
Morgan Hill, CA 95037

S&S Performance Products
Box 215
Viola, WI 54664

Stroker
engine parts

Tanks & fenders

Custom Chrome, Inc.
1 Jacqueline Court
Morgan HIll, CA 95037

Drag Specialties
9839 W. 69th St.
Eden Prairie, MN 55344

Tires

Avon Tires Ltd.
407 Howell Way
Edmonds, WA 98020

Continental Tire
1200 Wall Street West
Lyndhurst, NJ 07071

Michelin Tire Corp.
Patewood Executive Park
Box 19001
Greenville, SC 91324

Pirelli Tire Corp.
2001 Gateway Place #700
San Jose, CA 95110

Valves

F.C.C., Inc.
1220 Tangelo Terrace
Delray Beach, FL 33444

Rivera Engineering
6416 S. Western Ave.
Whittier, CA 90606

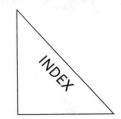